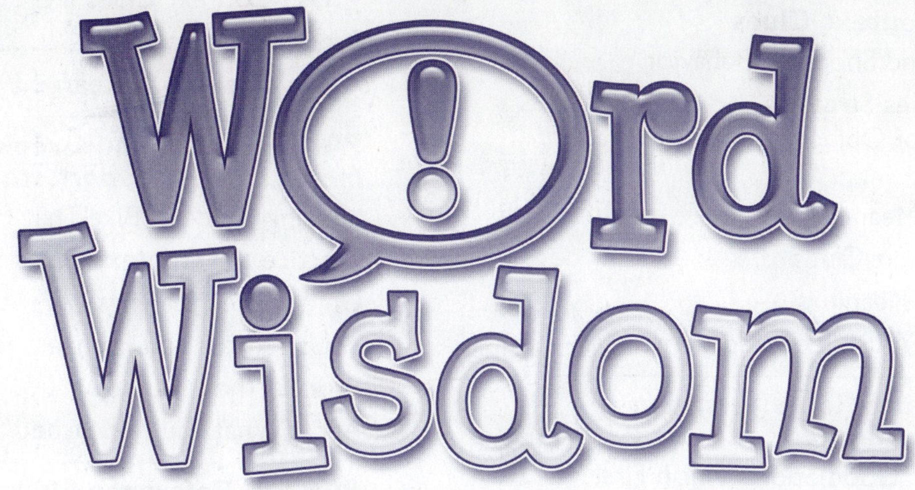


# Vocabulary for Listening, Speaking, Reading, and Writing

**Author**
## Jerry Zutell, Ph.D.
**The Ohio State University**

Credits: Located on last page of book

ISBN: 978-0-7367-9466-4

Copyright © 2013 Zaner-Bloser, Inc.


All rights reserved. No part of this book may be reproduced or transmitted in any form or by any means, electronic or mechanical, including photocopying, recording, or by any information storage and retrieval system, without permission in writing from the Publisher. The Publisher has made every effort to trace the ownership of all copyrighted material and to secure the necessary permissions to reprint these selections. In the event of any question arising as to the use of any material, the Publisher, while expressing regret for any inadvertent error, will be happy to make any necessary corrections.


Zaner-Bloser, Inc.
(1-800-421-3018)
www.zaner-bloser.com

# Contents

# Context Clues

*for Word Wisdom*

## Shoppers and Shopping Behavior

**Everyone shops. From the grocery store to the on-line catalog, choosing goods and services is a fact of everyday life. Yet nothing interests some researchers more than learning the factors that influence what we buy, when we buy, and where we buy.**

Whether you're shopping on-line, walking through a mall, or strolling down the grocery store aisles, retailers want to know all about you. A whole industry is devoted to **analyzing** exactly what you do in stores and why you do it. All around the country, shoppers' habits have already **affected** much of what you find in stores. By studying buying habits, retailers have turned stores into places where you'll want to spend more money.

What do retailers know about you? For one thing, they believe you're probably not unique. According to researchers, shoppers fall into categories by gender, by age group, and by other **factors**. As you might predict, male and female shoppers are quite different. For example, women generally get more pleasure out of the experience of shopping than men do. According to researchers, some women regard shopping as a form of **leisure,** often adding companionship or lunch to the experience. Women are more likely than men to take their time during the process. Many men, on the other hand, have a **tendency** to view shopping as an exercise or drill. In a store, they expect to advance in **lock step**. Their goal is to get to one specific department, find a specific item, make their purchase, and get out. Needless to say, these male and female shopping patterns don't go together. Researchers say that when men and women shop together, sales can go down!

Age also affects what people buy and where they buy it. Researchers know that people develop store loyalties. What better time to catch a consumer than when he or she is young?

When it comes to getting ready for different shoppers, retailers are **versatile,** all-around types who know how to create **inducements**. For example, some parents become **perturbed** while teens try on one item after another. They might leave the store if it were not for the comfortable chairs placed outside dressing rooms. Stores also make shopping carts and shopping bags handy. To encourage impulsive, **rash,** must-have-it-now buying on the part of teens, retailers play trendy music. They also create extremely attractive displays, often featuring teen models. Some stores hire teen sales assistants who look "just so" in the store's brand name clothing. Finally, since almost all shoppers tend to turn to the right when they enter a store, that's where retailers place the items they most want to sell.

# Context Clues Strategy

## Look for What Kind of Object, Concept, or Action the Word Is

**EXAMPLE:** José is a *convivial* boy who loves to talk and laugh with friends and go to social gatherings.

**CLUE:** The words *talk* and *laugh* are actions that help explain the word *convivial*. Social gatherings are things that would attract *convivial*, or friendly, people.

Here are the steps for using this context clues strategy to figure out the meaning of the word *lock step*.

**Read** the sentence with the unknown word and some of the sentences around it.

• • • • •

*Many men, on the other hand, have a **tendency** to view shopping as an exercise or drill. In a store, they expect to advance in **lock step**. Their goal is to get to one specific department, find a specific item, make their purchase, and get out.*

**Look** for context clues to the word's meaning. **What Kind of Object, Concept, or Action Is the Word?**

• • • • •

Exercises and drills are things people can do in *lock step*. The actions listed, *"to get to one specific department, find a specific item, make their purchase, and get out,"* suggest a set of steps that doesn't vary.

**Think** about the context clues and other information you may already know.

• • • • •

People often do drills and exercises in the same order every time. People learn the motions and then go through them mindlessly.

**Predict** a meaning for the word.

• • • • •

*Lock step* must describe something people do in a rigid way, without even thinking.

**Check** the Word Wisdom Dictionary to be sure of the meaning. Decide which of the meanings in the dictionary fits the context.

• • • • •

*Lock step* means "an inflexible procedure that cannot be changed."

**Practice the Strategy** Two of the boldfaced words from the article on page 6 are listed below. Using the context clues strategy on page 7, follow these steps to figure out the meanings of these words.

### affected

📖 **Read** the sentence that uses the word *affected* and some of the sentences around it.

🔍 **Look** for context clues to the word's meaning. **What Kind of Object, Concept, or Action Is the Word?**

_______________________________________________

💡 **Think** about the context clues. What other helpful information do you know?

_______________________________________________

➡️ **Predict** a meaning for the word *affected*.

_______________________________________________

✔️ **Check** your Word Wisdom Dictionary to be sure of the meaning for the word *affected*. Which of the meanings fits the context?

_______________________________________________

### factors

📖 **Read** the sentence that uses the word *factors* and some of the words and sentences around it.

🔍 **Look** for context clues to the word's meaning. **What Kind of Object, Concept, or Action Is the Word?**

_______________________________________________

💡 **Think** about the context clues. What other helpful information do you know?

_______________________________________________

➡️ **Predict** a meaning for the word *factors*.

_______________________________________________

✔️ **Check** your dictionary to be sure of the meaning for the word *factors*. Write the definition here.

_______________________________________________

analyze

✔ affect

✔ factor

leisure

tendency

✔ lock step

versatile

inducement

perturb

rash

**Use Context Clues** You have been introduced to three vocabulary words from the article on shopping behavior. Those words are checked off in the Word List here. Under "Vocabulary Word" below, write the other seven words from the Word List. Use context clues to predict a meaning for each word under "Your Prediction." Then check the meanings in the Word Wisdom Dictionary. Write the definition under "Dictionary Says."

| | Vocabulary Word | Your Prediction | Dictionary Says |
|---|---|---|---|
| 1 | | | |
| 2 | | | |
| 3 | | | |
| 4 | | | |
| 5 | | | |
| 6 | | | |
| 7 | | | |

**WORD LIST**

- analyze
- affect
- factor
- leisure
- tendency
- lock step
- versatile
- inducement
- perturb
- rash

**Choose the Correct Word** Write the word from the Word List that completes each sentence. You may need to add an ending to the word. Underline the part or parts of the sentence that helped you make your choice.

**1** Ashley spent her _______________ time listening to music and chatting with friends.

**2** Tim proved himself _______________ on the football field by running, throwing, and blocking well.

**3** Grades and activities are _______________ that colleges consider when admitting students.

**4** Jumping in that ice-cold water was a _______________ decision!

**5** Zach is so predictable. He does everything in _______________.

**6** The teacher promised shorter homework assignments as an _______________ to do well on the next test.

**7** When children don't listen, parents can become _______________.

**8** Two things doctors _______________ are blood tests and patient histories.

**9** Musical people have a _______________ to play instruments and go to concerts.

**10** I knew my suggestion had _______________ Sam's plans when he changed his schedule.

**Link to Your Life**  Follow the instructions and answer the questions below.

**1** Give two examples of something you **analyze**. _______________________

______________________________________________________________________

**2** Name two things you consider to be the opposite of **leisure**. ___________

______________________________________________________________________

**3** What is something you do in **lock step** at school or at home? ___________

______________________________________________________________________

**4** Give advice to a friend who has made **rash** decisions in the past.

______________________________________________________________________

**5** Name an **inducement** you could use to get a pet to behave. ___________

______________________________________________________________________

**6** If you are **versatile**, what might you do when one way of solving a problem doesn't work?

______________________________________________________________________

**7** Explain how a change at your school might **affect** your mood or your performance.

______________________________________________________________________

**8** Describe something that has **perturbed** you recently. ___________

______________________________________________________________________

**9** What **tendency** do you have that others admire? ___________

______________________________________________________________________

**10** What **factors** do you consider when deciding what to wear in the morning?

______________________________________________________________________

______________________________________________________________________

**Write It!**  Write an essay about one of the sentences above. Try to use several words from the Word List on page 10.

# Latin Roots

for Word Wisdom

## Playing Fair:
# Good Sports Finish First

- **You slide into second base—safe! Then the outfielder insists that he tagged you before you touched the base, and the umpire calls you out.**
- **A player on the other team scores a touchdown and dances around in the end zone, rubbing it in.**
- **At the end of a close game, players from the other team start calling you and your teammates names.**

If you have faced any of these situations, you were probably filled with anger and **turmoil**. How can you be a good sport when other players are behaving like this? In fact, how can you be a good sport when you see so much poor sportsmanship in professional sports? When winning means earning millions of dollars, players who are good sports seem to be hard to find. They might even be called names, sometimes by their own teammates.

However, no matter how **controversial** a call is, you need to remember that referees, umpires, and other officials are human and make mistakes, just like everyone else. Sometimes the errors are in favor of your **adversary,** and you are mightily tempted to question the official's eyesight, judgment, intelligence, and so on. Other times, the mistakes are in your team's favor—you don't argue about that, right?

Nevertheless, honesty and integrity have an important role in even the most **turbulent** competitions. Truly good athletes are not only **proficient** at their sport, but they also play fair at all times. Cheating, insulting opponents, and criticizing teammates are a few of the ways that poor sports announce their presence—and ruin the game.

If you are **disturbed** by this kind of behavior, go out of your way to be a good sport. That may seem like a **facile** suggestion, but your behavior can help counteract the negative behavior of others. You can become a positive role model.

If you are an **introvert** and feel uncomfortable stepping into a leadership role, you can lead quietly. You can provide extra encouragement to less talented players. Urge them not to be **perfectionists** who get upset over any little mistake. Help them strengthen the skills they need to improve their performance. Your support can give them confidence in themselves, which can lead to more confidence on the playing field.

If you are an **extrovert,** you might be a natural leader who can cheer noisily for your teammates—and applaud really good plays by the other team.

Don't forget to be a good sport when you are a spectator, too. Accept the referee's or umpire's call, and don't get upset by calls that seem misguided or mistaken. People who shout at officials, get extremely angry, boo the other team, and insult individual players add nothing to the game. These behaviors, however, indicate a great deal about their own character.

Being a good sport says a lot about your character, too. Win or lose, good sports always finish first.

**Practice the Context Clues Strategy**  Two of the boldfaced words from the selection on page 12 appear below. Use the context clues strategy that you learned in Part 1 on page 7 to figure out the meanings of the words.

## perfectionists

📖 **Read** the sentence that uses the word *perfectionists* and some of the sentences around it.

🔍 **Look** for context clues to the word's meaning. What tells you **What Kind of Object, Concept, or Action the Word Is?**

_______________________________________________

💡 **Think** about the context clues. What other helpful information do you know?

_______________________________________________

➡️ **Predict** a meaning for the word *perfectionist*.

_______________________________________________

✔️ **Check** your Word Wisdom Dictionary to be sure of the meaning of the word *perfectionist*. Write the definition here.

_______________________________________________

## extrovert

📖 **Read** the sentence that uses the word *extrovert* and some of the sentences around it.

🔍 **Look** for context clues to the word's meaning. What tells you **What Kind of Object, Concept, or Action the Word Is?**

_______________________________________________

💡 **Think** about the context clues. What other helpful information do you know?

_______________________________________________

➡️ **Predict** a meaning for the word *extrovert*.

_______________________________________________

✔️ **Check** your Word Wisdom Dictionary to be sure of the meaning of the word *extrovert*. Write the definition here.

_______________________________________________

Many English words come from Latin roots. Knowing the meanings of roots will help you unlock the meanings of many unknown words. Several words you studied in Part 1 have Latin roots. Each root is related to behavior.

| Latin Root: **vers, vert** | Latin Root: **fac, fect, fic** | Latin Root: **turb** |
|---|---|---|
| meaning: to turn | meaning: to make, to do, easy | meaning: turmoil |
| English word: *versatile* | English word: *factor* | English word: *perturb* |
| meaning: changing easily | meaning: ingredient, function | meaning: annoy, bother, agitate |

**Categorize by Roots** Find these roots in the Word List. Then write each word in the correct part of the tree. Think of other words you may know that come from the same Latin roots. Write them in the correct parts of the tree.

**WORD LIST**

- turmoil
- controversial
- adversary
- turbulent
- proficient
- disturb
- facile
- introvert
- perfectionist
- extrovert

Latin Root: **vers, vert**

Latin Root: **fac, fect, fic**

Latin Root: **turb**

**Behavior**

| Prefix | Meaning |
|--------|---------|
| intro- | inward |
| ad- | to, toward |
| contro- | against |
| dis- | apart, opposite of |
| extro- | outside, beyond |
| per- | through, completely |
| pro- | forward, in favor of |

**Example**

**intro-** (inward) + **vert** (turn) = **introvert**

**Use Roots and Prefixes** Circle any roots and prefixes you find in the boldfaced words below. Use context clues, roots, and prefixes to write the meaning of the word. Check your definitions in the Word Wisdom Dictionary.

**1** In the overcrowded school, the halls are filled with **turmoil**.

_____________________________________________

**2** Kelly is my best friend, but on the tennis court, she is my **adversary**.

_____________________________________________

**3** Alex's sleep was **disturbed** by the loud machinery outside his window.

_____________________________________________

**4** We did not expect such a quick, **facile** reply to such a hard question.

_____________________________________________

**5** The **introvert** sat alone in a corner during the party.

_____________________________________________

**6** Vick is such a **perfectionist**; he is impatient with others' mistakes.

_____________________________________________

**7** The new soccer field became **controversial** because some people argued that it would be too noisy and would increase traffic.

_____________________________________________

**8** A good writer, Sam is also **proficient** in math.

_____________________________________________

**9** With a storm coming, the captain didn't risk a voyage on the **turbulent** seas.

_____________________________________________

**10** The **extrovert** was the life of the party, talking and laughing with everyone.

_____________________________________________

**Complete the Analogy** Write the word from the Word List that best completes each analogy. You will have to add an ending to one word.

<table>
<tr><td>

**WORD LIST**

turmoil

controversial

adversary

turbulent

proficient

disturb

facile

introvert

perfectionist

extrovert

</td></tr>
</table>

**1** Smart : genius :: shy : _________________.

**2** Agreement : harmonious :: disagreement : _________________.

**3** Game : noise :: emergency : _________________.

**4** Delighted : unhappy :: content : _________________.

**5** Classroom : student :: party : _________________.

**6** Same : homogenous :: agitated : _________________.

**7** Brave : hero :: picky : _________________.

**8** High : low :: difficult : _________________.

**9** Friend : supporter :: enemy : _________________.

**10** Beginner : unskilled :: expert : _________________.

**Find Antonyms** Find words in the Word List that mean the opposite of the words in the left column. Write the antonyms in the right column.

| Words | Antonyms |
| --- | --- |
| **11** ally | |
| **12** outgoing | |
| **13** peace | |
| **14** settled | |
| **15** incompetent | |

**Complete the Word Continuum** A word continuum lists words in order from one extreme to another. For example, the words might be listed from simplest to most difficult. Write the words from the Word List on page 16 that best complete each row of words. The first one is done for you.

| | | |
|---|---|---|
| **1** beginning | intermediate | proficient |
| **2** stillness | activity | ________________ |
| **3** difficult | moderate | ________________ |
| **4** calm | ________________ | angry |
| **5** ________________ | slightly agitated | quiet |
| **6** ________________ | challenging | agreeable |

**Complete the Graphic Organizer** Write four nouns from the Word List on page 16 that name people.

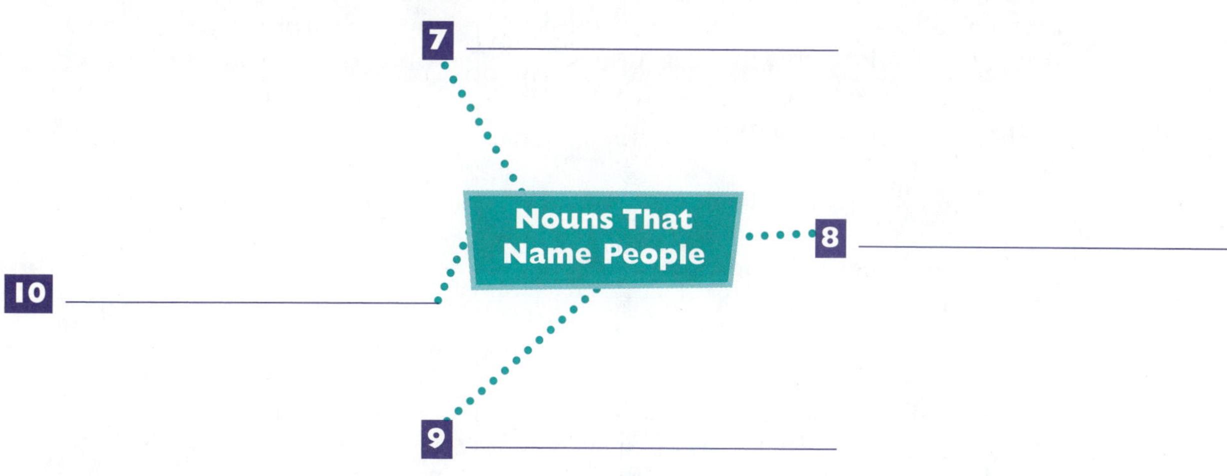

**Speak It!** Tell the class about two story characters who are extreme opposites. For example, describe one who is an introvert and one who is an extrovert. Use other Part 2 words in your descriptions.

# PART 3 Reference Skills

for Word Wisdom

## Making Friends:
## Fearless About Friendship

**Some people have a wide assortment of friends, and others have just one or two good friends, but nearly everyone could use a new friend.**

If you're the **amicable** type, you won't have any hesitations about going out and meeting new people. Your **exuberant** feelings just naturally attract people to you, like moths to a flame. You are fearless about making friends, an **intrepid,** confident, and successful adventurer into friendship.

However, many of us are not so fearless about friendship. We're concerned about being rejected by a potential new friend, a fear that can keep us paralyzed, friendship-wise. Perhaps a recent falling-out with a friend has left us **cynical** about the whole idea of friendship. Still, finding and making a new friend isn't that difficult. In fact, you can start small, without taking any huge emotional risks.

First of all, don't be **coy** about looking for a new friend. You should never feel embarrassed about trying to expand your circle of friends. You don't have to be **devious** about making friends either. The best approach is a straightforward one. You might begin simply by making sure you have a pleasant expression on your face. A bored, **irate,** or haughty expression will not encourage others to try to get to know you better.

Friendships often begin with shared interests. If you are a **fervent** game player, for example, locate others who share your passion. At the same time, don't look down on people who don't share this interest, as they might make perfectly good friends, too.

Along the same line, try not to gain a reputation as an **eccentric** person whose whole life revolves around one interest. The more interests you have, the more opportunities you have to make contact with potential friends. To develop a new interest, you might join a school or community club, audition for the school play, try out for the track or volleyball team, or take a course at the community center.

While you're exploring new interests, go out of your way to be a friend. Welcome new students to your school and help them feel comfortable and accepted. Offer to help carry things, volunteer for the clean-up committee, and just be kind to those around you in big and small ways. Hang around where other young people congregate and occasionally ask to join in games, trips to get pizza, or other activities. Think of some interesting activities and invite others to do them with you.

You don't have to be **flamboyant** in your efforts to find new friends. You might just ask an interesting person what he or she thinks about a homework assignment you both have. Compliment someone on a job well done, and you may end up deep in conversation with this person, well on your way to making a new friend. Soon you, too, will be fearless about friendship.

**Practice the Context Clues Strategy** Two of the boldfaced words from the selection on page 18 appear below. Use the context clues strategy you learned in Part 1 on page 7 to figure out the meanings of these words.

### intrepid

📖 **Read** the sentence that uses the word *intrepid* and some of the sentences around it.

🔍 **Look** for context clues to the word's meaning. What tells you **What Kind of Object, Concept, or Action the Word Is?**

_______________________________________________

💡 **Think** about the context clues. What other helpful information do you know?

_______________________________________________

➡️ **Predict** a meaning for the word *intrepid*.

_______________________________________________

✔️ **Check** your Word Wisdom Dictionary to be sure of the meaning of the word *intrepid*. Write the definition here.

_______________________________________________

### eccentric

📖 **Read** the sentence that uses the word *eccentric* and some of the sentences around it.

🔍 **Look** for context clues to the word's meaning. What tells you **What Kind of Object, Concept, or Action the Word Is?**

_______________________________________________

💡 **Think** about the context clues. What other helpful information do you know?

_______________________________________________

➡️ **Predict** a meaning for the word *eccentric*.

_______________________________________________

✔️ **Check** your Word Wisdom Dictionary to be sure of the meaning of the word *eccentric*. Which of the meanings for the word *eccentric* fits the context?

_______________________________________________

**Idioms and Special Dictionaries** An idiom is an expression with a special meaning. It cannot be understood from the meaning of each word. Look again at the essay on page 18. Read this sentence from paragraph 6. Can you find the idiom? Here's a part of that sentence:

*Hang around where other young people congregate....*

The phrase *hang around* is an idiom. Together, the words mean "to pass time or be around without any real purpose." You can check idioms in a special dictionary of idioms such as *A Dictionary of American Idioms.*

**Use a Dictionary of Idioms** Each idiom relates to a word in the Word List on page 21. Here are some common idioms about behavior. Decide on the meanings of the underlined idioms in these sentences. Rewrite the sentences on the lines using the words from the Word List in place of the idioms. Check your answers in an idiom dictionary.

**1** My dad became <u>hot under the collar</u> when he found out his new car was stolen.

_______________________________________

_______________________________________

**2** Cynthia <u>marches to the beat of a different drum</u>.

_______________________________________

**3** Uncle Joe always thinks everything will go wrong; his <u>glass is half empty</u>.

_______________________________________

_______________________________________

**4** They <u>jumped for joy</u> when their candidate won the election.

_______________________________________

**5** My mom says to <u>treat my neighbors as myself</u>.

_______________________________________

**Find the Meaning**

1. Use context clues.
2. Look for a familiar root, prefix, or suffix.
3. If the context or a word part doesn't help, check the dictionary.



**Define the Words** Follow the steps above to write the meaning of each boldfaced word. Write 1, 2, or 3 to show which steps you used.

**1** Tyrone was an **amicable** person whom everyone liked.

_______________________________________________

**2** The **eccentric** woman wore two different shoes.

_______________________________________________

**3** Max's **coy** behavior didn't fool me; I know he's actually very outgoing.

_______________________________________________

**4** The furious look on the man's face told us he was **irate**.

_______________________________________________

**5** The crook used **devious** means to find out when people left their homes.

_______________________________________________

**6** She laughed and danced, unable to contain her **exuberant** feelings.

_______________________________________________

**7** The **flamboyant** costume was red and gold and full of ruffles.

_______________________________________________

**8** In Jen's **cynical** view of people, everyone is dishonest.

_______________________________________________

**9** An **intrepid** hiker, Anna kept going on the trail in spite of the danger.

_______________________________________________

**10** Ryan is a **fervent** believer in exercise; he jogs five miles every day.

_______________________________________________

**WORD LIST**

- amicable
- exuberant
- intrepid
- cynical
- coy
- devious
- irate
- fervent
- eccentric
- flamboyant

**Match the Synonyms** Write the vocabulary word that means the same or nearly the same as each synonym listed below.

| Synonym | Vocabulary Word |
|---|---|
| 1 friendly | |
| 2 brave | |
| 3 high-spirited | |
| 4 shy | |
| 5 underhanded | |
| 6 odd | |
| 7 bitter | |
| 8 angry | |
| 9 showy | |
| 10 passionate | |

# Apply What You've Learned

**Demonstrate Word Knowledge** Answer the question or follow the directions.

**1** What might an **eccentric** person do while walking down the street?

_______________________________________________

**2** Describe a **flamboyant** style of clothing.

_______________________________________________

**3** Describe someone who has an **irate** look on his or her face.

_______________________________________________

**4** Give an example of something you might do in a **fervent** way.

_______________________________________________

**5** Name one thing that can make you feel **exuberant**.

_______________________________________________

**Use Connotations** Many words have a positive or a negative connotation, or implied meaning. Decide on the connotation of the words *irate, cynical, amicable, intrepid,* and *devious.* Write these words in the chart under the proper heading. Add other words you know to complete each column.

| Positive Words | Negative Words |
| --- | --- |
|  |  |
|  |  |
|  |  |
|  |  |
|  |  |

**Write It!** Write a paragraph describing a person with the positive words in the left column. Write a paragraph describing a person with the negative words in the right column. Which person would you rather have as a friend? Why?

# Review


**Categorize by Syllables and Identify Latin Roots** Sort the words in the Word List according to the number of syllables in each word. After you write each word in the correct column, draw a line through that word in the Word List. Then circle the roots *vers*, *vert*, *fac*, *fect*, *fic*, and *turb* as you find them in some words.

## WORD LIST

- analyze
- affect
- factor
- leisure
- tendency
- lock step
- versatile
- inducement
- perturb
- rash
- turmoil
- controversial
- adversary
- turbulent
- proficient
- disturb
- facile
- introvert
- perfectionist
- extrovert
- amicable
- exuberant
- intrepid
- cynical
- coy
- devious
- irate
- fervent
- eccentric
- flamboyant

| One or Two Syllables | Three Syllables | Four or More Syllables |
|---|---|---|
| | | |

**Choose the Antonym** Write a word from the Word List on page 24 that is an antonym—or opposite—for the word below.

**1** friend _________________________

**2** trusting _________________________

**3** cowardly _________________________

**4** well-planned _________________________

**5** ordinary _________________________

**Choose the Synonym** Write a word from the Word List on page 24 that is a synonym for the word below.

**6** crafty _________________________

**7** skilled _________________________

**8** angry _________________________

**9** interpret _________________________

**10** inclination _________________________

**Complete the Sentences** Choose a word from the Word List on page 24 to complete each sentence.

**11** I like to spend my _________________________ time painting.

**12** The soldiers marched in _________________________.

**13** The economy will _________________________ the outcome of the election.

**14** Good grades are an _________________________ to do your work.

**15** The flashy, _________________________ dancer dressed in red and gold glitter.

# Taking Vocabulary Tests

**TEST-TAKING STRATEGY**

Some vocabulary tests ask you to choose the meaning of a word in a short phrase. Because you will have several choices, it is important to read them all. Never select a meaning until you are sure it is the very best meaning given.

**Sample:**

an <u>affluent</u> person
- ○ flowing
- ○ affected
- ○ friendly
- ● rich

**Practice Test**   Fill in the circle for the word or words that have the SAME or ALMOST THE SAME meaning as the underlined word.

**1** <u>affected</u> the outcome
- ○ ignored
- ○ delayed
- ○ influenced
- ○ guaranteed

**2** the <u>turbulent</u> air
- ○ calm
- ○ polluted
- ○ clear
- ○ agitated

**3** <u>disturbed</u> the sleeping baby
- ○ picked up
- ○ avoided
- ○ bothered
- ○ soothed

**4** the <u>exuberant</u> child
- ○ lively
- ○ timid
- ○ bright
- ○ frightened

**5** a <u>coy</u> smile
- ○ mysterious
- ○ unusual
- ○ pleasant
- ○ shy

**6** <u>perturbed</u> the counselor
- ○ relieved
- ○ greatly upset
- ○ worried
- ○ excited

**7** the <u>versatile</u> performer
- ○ all-around
- ○ comic
- ○ musical
- ○ inexperienced

**8** a well-known <u>extrovert</u>
- ○ shy person
- ○ outgoing person
- ○ scared person
- ○ religious person

**9** the <u>lock step</u> routine
- ○ safe
- ○ walking
- ○ long
- ○ unchanging

**10** offer the <u>inducement</u>
- ○ explanation
- ○ punishment
- ○ benefit
- ○ option

**Use Suffixes** The suffix *-ly* makes a word an adverb. Use this suffix to make new words from *fervent, flamboyant, leisure, coy,* and *amicable.* You will need to change one spelling. Then write a sentence using each of the new words.

| Word | + Suffix | = New Word | Sentence |
|---|---|---|---|
| fervent | | | |
| flamboyant | | | |
| leisure | | | |
| coy | | | |
| amicable | | | |

**Speak It!** Start making a habit of using the new words you learn each week. Describe a place where people behave in many different ways, such as at a football stadium, while driving on the highway, or at a party. Use as many of the words from this Behavior unit as you can.

# Context Clues

for Word Wisdom

## How's the Weather?
# The Science of Forecasting

**Will the game be rained out? What should I wear today? Do I need to bring my bike inside? To answer these questions, we rely on weather reports. Predicting the weather is a complicated process, however. It relies on thousands of measurements taken all over the world.**

When it comes to the weather, it's useful to know what is ahead. In order to **gauge** the weather, people have always looked to the skies for signs of rain and snow. Formal attempts to understand the weather go back at least as far as ancient Greece. Then, **forecasts** were used to help with important decisions about everything from planting crops to going to battle. They were, however, much less accurate than they are now.

Accurate forecasts became possible in the 1800s. Tools for measuring and collecting data from faraway places were developed. Because weather events are connected, data from one place give, at best, only a **partial** picture. For the complete **extent** of the weather picture, data are needed from all over the world.

What data do meteorologists use? They use air pressure readings, air temperature measurements, and measurements of wind force and direction. Humidity readings on the surface of the Earth as well as at other **altitudes** are important, too. All these data contribute to an overall picture of conditions and help scientists plot and predict the movement of weather systems.

Various tools are used to gather this information. Thermometers measure air temperature. **Barometers** have long been used to determine air pressure. Wind-measurement instruments are also common.

Data used in forecasting come from all over the globe. Satellites gather some of it by means of photographs and other devices. Airplanes, ships, floating weather stations, and weather balloons also play a role by carrying equipment that **monitors** the weather. Radio transmitters, hooked up to weather-measuring devices, send the data to computers, which **consolidate** and analyze it. This results in computer-generated maps and predictions.

When viewers turn on a television weather report, they hear a report and see a map. **Standard** figures and symbols are used to show specific kinds of weather patterns on the weather map and help viewers understand the forecast. These maps show precipitation and weather fronts where two different air **masses** meet.

Weather forecasts are reasonably accurate for periods of approximately 12 to 72 hours.



Measurement · UNIT 2

# Context Clues Strategy

## Look for What the Word Is Used For

**EXAMPLE:** Rachel used the *protractor* to measure the angle.

**CLUE:** The phrase *to measure the angle* tells what a *protractor* is used for. A protractor is an instrument or tool for measuring angles.

Here are the steps for using this context clues strategy to figure out the meaning of the word *forecast*.

**Read** the sentence with the unknown word and some of the sentences around it.

*Formal attempts to understand the weather go back at least as far as ancient Greece. Then, **forecasts** were used to help with important decisions about everything from planting crops to going to battle.*

**Look** for context clues to the word's meaning. What clues about **What the Word Is Used For** can you find?

The sentences say that ancient Greeks had *formal attempts to understand the weather* and that forecasts were used *to help with decisions* about all kinds of things.

**Think** about the context clues and other information you may already know.

I know that I often make decisions about what to do based on what I think the weather will be like.

**Predict** a meaning for the word.

A *forecast* is an attempt to predict something, like the weather.

**Check** your Word Wisdom Dictionary to be sure of the meaning. Decide which of the meanings in the dictionary fits with the context.

In this context, the word *forecast* means "a prediction."

**Practice the Strategy** Two of the words from the essay on page 28 are used in this activity. Use the context clues strategy on page 29 to figure out the meaning of each word.

## barometers

📖 **Read** the sentence that uses the word *barometers* and some of the sentences around it.

🔍 **Look** for context clues to the word's meaning. What clues to **What the Word Is Used For** can you find?

_______________________________________________

💡 **Think** about the context clues. What other information do you know?

_______________________________________________

➡ **Predict** a meaning for the word *barometer*.

_______________________________________________

✔ **Check** your Word Wisdom Dictionary to be sure of the meaning for the word *barometer*.

_______________________________________________

## standard

📖 **Read** the sentence that uses the word *standard* and some of the sentences around it.

🔍 **Look** for context clues to the word's meaning. What clues to **What the Word Is Used For** can you find?

_______________________________________________

💡 **Think** about the context clues. What other information do you know?

_______________________________________________

➡ **Predict** a meaning for the word *standard*.

_______________________________________________

✔ **Check** your Word Wisdom Dictionary to be sure of the meaning for the word *standard*.

_______________________________________________

**Use Context Clues** You have been introduced to three vocabulary words from the weather essay. Those words are checked off in the Word List here. Under "Vocabulary Word" below, write the other words from the Word List. Predict a meaning for each word under "Your Prediction." Then check the meanings in the Word Wisdom Dictionary. Write the definition under "Dictionary Says."

**WORD LIST**

- gauge
- ✔ forecast
- partial
- extent
- altitude
- ✔ barometer
- monitor
- consolidate
- ✔ standard
- mass

| | Vocabulary Word | Your Prediction | Dictionary Says |
|---|---|---|---|
| 1 | | | |
| 2 | | | |
| 3 | | | |
| 4 | | | |
| 5 | | | |
| 6 | | | |
| 7 | | | |

**WORD LIST**

gauge

forecast

partial

extent

altitude

barometer

monitor

consolidate

standard

mass

**Find the Antonyms**  Write the word from the Word List that is an antonym—or opposite—for the underlined word in each sentence.

**1** The last step in the process is to <u>separate</u> all the measurements.

_________________________

**2** We plan to <u>ignore</u> changing temperatures in the Pacific Ocean.

_________________________

**3** This book gives a <u>complete</u> explanation of how to convert those

measurements. _________________________

**4** We measured the <u>depth</u> through the use of special instruments.

_________________________

**Choose the Correct Word**  Write the word from the Word List that best completes each sentence.

**5** All weather stations use certain _________________________ instruments to collect data.

**6** The weather map showed that a cold air _________________________ was heading in our direction.

**7** An outdoor thermometer allows me to _________________________ the temperature outside.

**8** According to his reading of the _________________________, we are in a high-pressure system.

**9** The day after the tornado, the officials had to measure the

_________________________ of the damage.

**10** According to the latest _________________________, there are several sunny, warm days ahead this week.

# Apply What You've Learned



**Find Examples**   Only one sentence in each pair below uses the boldfaced word correctly. Write **correct** next to the example that is correct.

**1** The **extent** snowfall can be measured. ____________

The **extent** of the snowfall can be measured. ____________

**2** Lisa will **monitor** and record cloud movement today. ____________

Lisa will **monitor** the book about cloud movement. ____________

**3** The **forecast** suggests that precipitation is on the way. ____________

The **forecast** shows that last year we had an unusually high level of

precipitation. ____________

**4** The measurement was taken at several **altitudes**. ____________

The measurement was taken by several **altitudes**. ____________

**5** After we **consolidate** the data, we can gather it. ____________

After we **consolidate** the data, we can analyze it. ____________

**6** Most weather measurements are recorded in **standard** units. ____________

Most **standard** measurements vary. ____________

**7** Accurate predictions result from **partial** information. ____________

Inaccurate predictions result from **partial** information. ____________

**8** **Barometers** measure air pressure. ____________

**Barometers** measure length. ____________

**9** Gathering clouds formed a **mass** on the horizon. ____________

Scattering clouds formed a **mass** on the horizon. ____________

**10** Meteorologists **gauge** the wind speeds of a hurricane. ____________

Meteorologists speed up the hurricane **gauge**. ____________

**Write It!**   Imagine you work at a weather station. Write about your job. Use as many of the words from the Word List on page 32 as you can.

# PART 2

# Latin and Greek Roots

## Buying Guide:
## A Bike That Fits

**Buying a bicycle used to be easy— when stores offered only a few choices. Now bikes are available in a wide range of types, sizes, and brands, and you can even have a bike tailor-made just for you. So how can you decide which bike to buy?**

Before you select a bike, you need to consider the kind of riding you will do. Will this bike be your major form of transportation? Or will you just ride it occasionally, venturing no farther than the **perimeter** of your neighborhood? Will you spend a **substantial** part of your riding time on pavement, dirt paths, or mountain trails? Will you be sharing the bike with a sibling or a friend? In that case, you might **apportion** the time each of you will use the bike and factor your different needs into your buying decision.

The size of the bike affects your safety, comfort, and enjoyment. A bike that is **disproportionate** for you might be too tall, or its seat might be set back too far from the handlebars. The staff at a bike store should be able to help you select a bike that fits the length of both your legs and your upper body.

A larger bike might require you to stretch to reach the handlebars, but if you like to ride leaning forward, this should not pose a problem. For example, the seat does not have to be **equidistant** from

both wheels—if you prefer, the seat could be placed closer to the back wheel.

In most bike stores, the men's and women's bikes are together with no **partition** separating them. Customers are encouraged to consider both types of bike. In fact, a tall woman might be more comfortable on a bike with a crossbar. A man who feels more comfortable on a bike without a crossbar should purchase the bike that suits him best.

As you consider bike accessories, be sure to get a helmet, and be sure to wear it while you are biking. **Statistics** show that a helmet can lower your risk of a serious head injury by eighty-five percent. You might also want to purchase a speedometer to measure your speed and an **odometer** to measure the distance you travel. Just as runners can use **pedometers** to measure how far they run, bikers can use odometers.

The last step before you make a purchase is a practice ride, of course. You should be able to get on and off the bike easily and comfortably. As you ride the bike, there should be no pull to the right or left to ruin the **symmetry** of the balance. You should feel in control at all times.

Now you're prepared to visit a bike store and explore the many options. With some thought and planning, you will find a bike that is just right for you and your needs. Enjoy the ride!

## partition

**Read** the sentence that uses the word *partition* and some of the sentences around it.

**Look** for context clues to the word's meaning. What clues about **What the Word Is Used For** can you find?

_________________________________________________

**Think** about the context clues. What other information do you know?

_________________________________________________

**Predict** a meaning for the word *partition*.

_________________________________________________

**Check** your Word Wisdom Dictionary to be sure of the meaning of the word *partition*. Write the definition here.

_________________________________________________

## odometer

**Read** the sentence that uses the word *odometer* and some of the sentences around it.

**Look** for context clues to the word's meaning. What clues about **What the Word Is Used For** can you find?

_________________________________________________

**Think** about the context clues. What other information do you know?

_________________________________________________

**Predict** a meaning for the word *odometer*.

_________________________________________________

**Check** your Word Wisdom Dictionary to be sure of the meaning of the word *odometer*. Write the definition here.

_________________________________________________

Many English words have Latin or Greek roots. Knowing the meanings of roots can help you understand the meanings of many words. Many of the words you studied in Part 1 have Latin or Greek roots. Each root below is related to measurement.

| | | |
|---|---|---|
| Latin and Greek Root: **meter, metr** <br> meaning: measure <br> English word: *barometer* <br> meaning: an instrument for measuring air pressure | Latin Root: **part, port** <br> meaning: a share or part <br> English word: *partial* <br> meaning: not complete | Latin Root: **sta** <br> meaning: to stand <br> English word: *standard* <br> meaning: usual or customary |

**WORD LIST**

- perimeter
- substantial
- apportion
- disproportionate
- equidistant
- partition
- statistics
- odometer
- pedometer
- symmetry

**Categorize by Roots**   Write each word from the Word List in alphabetical order in the column below. Circle the root in each word. Think of other words that have the same roots as the words in each column. Add them to the correct group.

## Measurement

| Latin and Greek Root: **meter, metr** | Latin Root: **part, port** | Latin Root: **sta** |
|---|---|---|
| __________ | __________ | __________ |
| __________ | __________ | __________ |
| __________ | __________ | __________ |
| __________ | __________ | __________ |
| __________ | __________ | __________ |

| Prefix | Meaning | Example |
|---|---|---|
| peri- | around, enclosing | **peri-** (around) + **meter** (measure) = **perimeter** |
| dis- | not, opposite of | |
| equi- | equal | |

**Use Roots and Prefixes**   Circle any roots and prefixes you find in the boldfaced words below. Use context clues, roots, and prefixes to write the meaning of the word. Check your definitions in your Word Wisdom Dictionary.

**1** The **perimeter** of our yard determines how much fence we need.

_______________________________________________

**2** We planted the trees so they would be **equidistant** to each other.

_______________________________________________

**3** By placing the same number and size windows on each side of the door, the architect created **symmetry**.

_______________________________________________

**4** The company uses accident **statistics** to determine insurance costs.

_______________________________________________

**5** Our class has a **disproportionate** number of boys.

_______________________________________________

**6** The **odometer** showed that we had traveled 149 miles.

_______________________________________________

**7** Mike's **pedometer** showed that he had walked six miles.

_______________________________________________

**8** Emergency supplies were **apportioned** according to the size of each family.

_______________________________________________

**9** The tornado caused **substantial** damage to the towns in its path.

_______________________________________________

**10** Let's use a **partition** to divide the room into two parts.

_______________________________________________

WORD LIST

perimeter

substantial

apportion

disproportionate

equidistant

partition

statistics

odometer

pedometer

symmetry


**Use the Words Correctly in Writing**   Rewrite each sentence in your own words. Use the word in parentheses in your sentence.

**1** When we remove that divider, our meeting space will double. (partition)

___________________________________________

**2** The detectives walked all around the building looking for clues. (perimeter)

___________________________________________

**3** Everything about the design was carefully planned to create exact balance and harmony. (symmetry)

___________________________________________

___________________________________________

**4** The trip to Los Angeles was almost 1,600 miles. (odometer)

___________________________________________

___________________________________________

**5** This year has been unusual for the amount of rain that has fallen. (disproportionate)

___________________________________________

**6** Our walk to the library was 1.5 miles. (pedometer)

___________________________________________

**7** I ate quite a bit of food at that party! (substantial)

___________________________________________

**8** Hasn't the theory been shown to be inaccurate? (statistics)

___________________________________________

**9** I tried measuring both paths to see which was longer. (equidistant)

___________________________________________

**10** On the last day of the hike, the four of us had to be careful about our remaining water supply. (apportion)

___________________________________________

___________________________________________

# Apply What You've Learned

**Demonstrate Word Knowledge**  Answer each question.

**1** How might you create **symmetry** in a garden?

_______________________________________________

**2** When might you look at your **odometer**?

_______________________________________________

**3** Why would some people carry a **pedometer**?

_______________________________________________

**4** What could you do with a **partition**?

_______________________________________________

**5** To build a wall around your yard, why should you know its **perimeter**?

_______________________________________________

**Complete the Sentences**  Complete each sentence below.

**6** The two locations were **equidistant** because

_______________________________________________

**7** I saved a **substantial** amount by

_______________________________________________

**8** The food was **apportioned** according to

_______________________________________________

**9** Nicole's share of the work was **disproportionate** because

_______________________________________________

**10** **Statistics** from the election showed that

_______________________________________________

**Speak It!**  Work with a partner to discuss these questions, using as many of the vocabulary words from this part as you can.
- *When do you use measurements or statistics in your daily life?*
- *Why would you use a pedometer or an odometer?*

# PART 3 Reference Skills

*for Word Wisdom*

## Drought: Not Enough Water

**Drought is a normal feature of climate, and it occurs almost everywhere. Chances are, you've experienced drought in your region of the country.**

A *drought* is a drier-than-normal condition that results in water-related problems. When little or no rain falls in a region, the soil dries out and crops and other plants suffer. If this condition continues for weeks, months, or years, water levels in streams, rivers, and lakes begin to fall. The dry period then becomes a drought.

Rainfall in different regions varies from **scanty** to **copious**. Meteorologists keep records to determine the average annual rainfall. In the deserts of the Southwestern United States, the yearly rainfall might be only three inches. In contrast, the rain forests of the American Northwest receive more than 150 inches of rain a year. The rainfall in your region is probably somewhere in between.

With the normal variations in rainfall, it's difficult to determine when a drought begins. A long period may pass before the problem is evident. In addition, a humid climate can offset a **moderate** decrease in rainfall. Also, less water evaporates during cool, cloudy weather, conserving the available water. Even if rainfall is average for a certain year, a dry period at planting time or soon after can present a problem for farmers.

When a drought occurs, people are often limited to a small **ration** of water as a way to share this resource fairly. That ration might be increased or decreased in **increments,** based on the rainfall—or lack of rainfall—during that period. Towns and cities may set rules controlling when residents can water their lawns and wash their cars, for example. Deciding how to **allocate** scarce water to all who need it is a complex decision. Many different needs must be balanced. Local, state, and federal agencies work together to decide how our needs for water will be met.

If a drought occurs, water might be diverted from streams and rivers to irrigate crops or generate power. However, a **multitude** of problems can **accrue** from this approach. First, this diversion causes the water supply to **dwindle** for people who live downstream. Lower water levels in lakes, rivers, and reservoirs can also affect the fish and wildlife that depend on water to survive. When wetlands dry out, this valuable habitat can be **decimated**. Many communities also depend on the electricity that is generated by dams. Lower water levels can affect this power supply.

During a drought, cooperation is the key. Everyone must work together to deal with the problem. For example, farmers can change their irrigation practices so they use just enough water to sustain their crops. Repeated droughts in a region may indicate a need to plant crops that require less water. Cities and towns can ration water to their residents. Factories can evaluate their manufacturing processes to find ways to conserve water.

With everyone saving a little water, enough will be available to meet our critical needs until the rains return.

**Practice the Context Clues Strategy** Here are two of the boldfaced words from the essay on page 40. Use the context clues strategy you learned in Part 1 on page 29 to figure out the meanings of these words.

## ration

**Read** the sentence that uses the word *ration* and some of the sentences around it.

**Look** for context clues to the word's meaning. What clues about **What the Word Is Used For** can you find?

______________________________________________

**Think** about the context clues. What other information do you know?

______________________________________________

**Predict** a meaning for the word *ration*.

______________________________________________

**Check** your Word Wisdom Dictionary to be sure of the meaning of the word *ration*. Which of the meanings for the word *ration* fits the context?

______________________________________________

## allocate

**Read** the sentence that uses the word *allocate* and some of the sentences around it.

**Look** for context clues to the word's meaning. What clues about **What the Word Is Used For** can you find?

______________________________________________

**Think** about the context clues. What other information do you know?

______________________________________________

**Predict** a meaning for the word *allocate*.

______________________________________________

**Check** your Word Wisdom Dictionary to be sure of the meaning of the word *allocate*. Write the definition here.

______________________________________________

## Using a Thesaurus for Multiple Meanings

A **thesaurus** is a reference book that lists synonyms and antonyms. When substituting a synonym from a thesaurus, be sure to pay attention to multiple parts of speech and the multiple meanings of words. Here are several meanings and synonyms for *moderate*.

**moderate**

| Meaning | Synonyms |
|---|---|
| reasonable (adj.) | modest, sensible, restrained, fair |
| average (adj.) | medium, normal, fair, mediocre |
| curb (v.) | control, diminish, restrain, regulate |
| arbitrate (v.) | mediate, referee, control |

Which meaning or synonym could be substituted for the word *moderate* in this sentence?

*Doctors recommend proper nutrition, along with moderate exercise.*

The words *reasonable, sensible, medium,* and *normal* could all be used instead of *moderate*. However, the words *mediocre, restrain, regulate, mediate, control,* and *referee* wouldn't make sense in this sentence.

**Use a Thesaurus**   Look up the boldfaced word in a thesaurus, and list as many appropriate synonyms as you can, keeping in mind the part of speech and meaning of the word.

**1** The first nationwide tour by the new band drew a **multitude** of fans.

_______________________________________________

**2** If I do all my work and study, my grades will go up by **increments**.

_______________________________________________

**3** During war, food sometimes must be **rationed** to prevent famine.

_______________________________________________

**4** This term paper will require **copious** amounts of research.

_______________________________________________

**Find the Meaning**

1. Use context clues.
2. Look for a familiar root, prefix, or suffix.
3. If the context or a word part doesn't help, check the dictionary.

**WORD LIST**

scanty

copious

moderate

ration

increment

allocate

multitude

accrue

dwindle

decimate

**Define the Words**   Follow the steps above to decide on the meaning of each boldfaced word. Write the meaning of the word. Then write 1, 2, or 3 to show which steps you used.

**1** Because the wood supply was **scanty**, they built their homes of grass.

_______________________________________________________

**2** The **ration** consisted of a pound of flour, some cheese, and three eggs.

_______________________________________________________

**3** Jorge wasn't very hungry, so he ate just a **moderate** amount of food.

_______________________________________________________

**4** Did they **allocate** the pencils and paper to the students in a fair way?

_______________________________________________________

**5** As Marta bought more new clothes, she watched her savings **dwindle**.

_______________________________________________________

**6** Honors **accrue** to players who play well and exemplify sportsmanship.

_______________________________________________________

**7** Six suitcases is a **copious** amount of luggage for a two-week trip.

_______________________________________________________

**8** The **multitude** of questions made the information session very long.

_______________________________________________________

**9** A huge hurricane could **decimate** our coastline.

_______________________________________________________

**10** Over the years, the office manager saw her salary increase by small **increments**.

_______________________________________________________

**WORD LIST**

- scanty
- copious
- moderate
- ration
- increment
- allocate
- multitude
- accrue
- dwindle
- decimate

**Classify the Synonyms** Add the correct word from the Word List to each group. You can check your synonyms using a thesaurus.

1. portion, share, part, ___________________________

2. gather, accumulate, collect, ___________________________

3. reasonable, measured, average, ___________________________

4. increase, addition, step, ___________________________

5. diminish, lessen, reduce, ___________________________

6. divide, distribute, partition, ___________________________

7. small, limited, meager, ___________________________

8. plentiful, abundant, huge, ___________________________

9. crowd, many, throng, ___________________________

10. destroy, ruin, end, ___________________________

**Relate the Meanings** Use what you have learned about the boldfaced words to follow the directions or answer the questions.

**1** List some things you have **accrued** in your home over the last several years.

______________________________________________

**2** Name some things that might need to be **rationed** in an emergency.

______________________________________________

**3** What could **decimate** a forest?

______________________________________________

**4** How fast would you be going if your car were traveling at a **moderate** speed?

______________________________________________

**5** If someone ate a **copious** amount of ice cream, how much would that be?

______________________________________________

**6** If you counted in **increments** of 2, list the numbers you would say from 20 to 30.

______________________________________________

**7** Where would you find a **multitude** of books?

______________________________________________

**8** How would you **allocate** the use of one computer among four people?

______________________________________________

**9** Name some natural resources that are **dwindling**.

______________________________________________

**10** What would be the result of a **scanty** amount of rain?

______________________________________________

**Write It!** Imagine that a very poor country suffers an extreme drought, and crops fail due to lack of water. Describe how the drought affects the crops and how this affects the country's food supply. Describe what actions the government might take. Use as many of the vocabulary words from Part 3 as you can.

# Review

**Label It** Complete the caption for each drawing with the correct words from the Word List.

## WORD LIST

- gauge
- forecast
- partial
- extent
- altitude
- barometer
- monitor
- consolidate
- standard
- mass
- perimeter
- substantial
- apportion
- disproportionate
- equidistant
- partition
- statistics
- odometer
- pedometer
- symmetry
- scanty
- copious
- moderate
- ration
- increment
- allocate
- multitude
- accrue
- dwindle
- decimate

**A**



The ________________

shows a

________________

number of miles.

**B**

Devices on the weather balloon

________________ the air

temperature and

________________ other

conditions at varying

________________ .

**C**

Shoshanna wanted to divide a room with a

________________ . If it is

________________ from

both ends of the room, the

________________ of

each part of the room will be

48 feet.

**D**

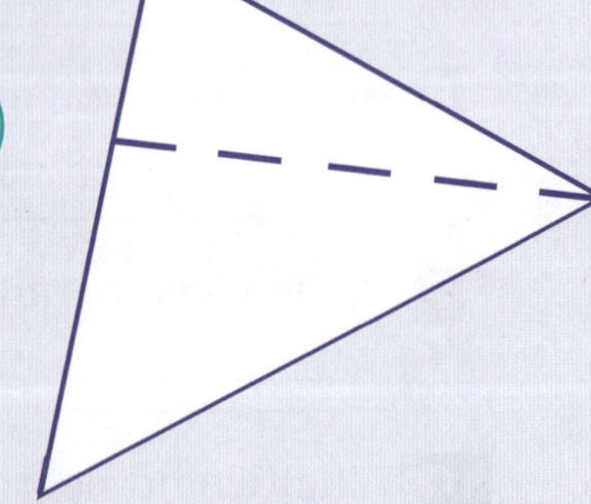

The shapes created from the triangle do not have

________________ ;

one part of the triangle is

________________ to

the other.

**Check the Meaning**   If the underlined word is used correctly, write **correct**. If the underlined word is used incorrectly, write **incorrect**.

**1** The cloud <u>mass</u> appeared to be moving slowly.

**2** Henry used his <u>pedometer</u> to measure angles.

**3** Not much interest <u>accrues</u> in a checking account.

**4** The <u>barometer</u> showed the outdoor temperature.

**5** As the rain continued, our chances for holding the picnic <u>dwindled</u>.

**Choose the Correct Word**   Write the word from the Word List that completes each sentence. You may need to change the ending of a word.

**6** The surprise attack ＿＿＿＿＿＿＿＿＿＿ the resistance troops.

**7** A ＿＿＿＿＿＿＿＿＿＿ of problems forced Rosa to rethink her plans.

**8** The bank let me ＿＿＿＿＿＿＿＿＿＿ my payments so that I could write just one check.

**9** The weather map showed the ＿＿＿＿＿＿＿＿＿＿ of the storm's reach.

**10** A ＿＿＿＿＿＿＿＿＿＿ amount of rain will promote plant growth without flooding the roots.

**11** A ＿＿＿＿＿＿＿＿＿＿ divided the two rooms.

**12** The hikers had to ＿＿＿＿＿＿＿＿＿＿ their water supply.

**13** A huge ＿＿＿＿＿＿＿＿＿＿ of ice floated by the ocean liner.

**14** The doctors will ＿＿＿＿＿＿＿＿＿＿ my blood pressure.

**15** Tony loved his probabilities and ＿＿＿＿＿＿＿＿＿＿ class.

# Taking Vocabulary Tests

### TEST-TAKING STRATEGY

Not all vocabulary tests are the same! Take a moment to look over the entire test before you begin. Be sure to read the sample item. Begin the test only when you are sure you know what you are being asked to do. One thing the test might ask you to do is choose a word that means the same as a boldfaced word. If it does, be sure to read all possible answers before you decide.

**Sample:**

a **simple** math problem
- Ⓐ long
- Ⓑ easy
- Ⓒ difficult
- Ⓓ pleasant

**Practice Test**   Fill in the letter of the answer that means **the same** or **nearly the same** as the boldfaced word in each phrase.

**1** incorrect **gauge**
- Ⓐ answer
- Ⓑ measure
- Ⓒ thinking
- Ⓓ experiment

**2** each **increment** of 10 m.p.h.
- Ⓐ part
- Ⓑ ratio
- Ⓒ speedometer reading
- Ⓓ added amount

**3** **scanty** amount
- Ⓐ huge
- Ⓑ tiny
- Ⓒ satisfactory
- Ⓓ decreasing

**4** **apportion** the supplies
- Ⓐ hide
- Ⓑ divide
- Ⓒ get rid of
- Ⓓ partly increase

**5** **forecast** the chance of rain
- Ⓐ predict
- Ⓑ discuss
- Ⓒ argue over
- Ⓓ decide

**6** **allocate** the funds
- Ⓐ spend
- Ⓑ invest
- Ⓒ distribute
- Ⓓ double

**7** a **partial** reassurance
- Ⓐ complete
- Ⓑ incomplete
- Ⓒ friendly
- Ⓓ sympathetic

**8** the **copious** amount of data
- Ⓐ curious
- Ⓑ insufficient
- Ⓒ doubtful
- Ⓓ huge

**9** the soldier's **ration**
- Ⓐ uniform
- Ⓑ arms
- Ⓒ share
- Ⓓ medals

**10** at the **standard** rate
- Ⓐ usual
- Ⓑ current
- Ⓒ reduced
- Ⓓ bargain

**Word Fractions**  Use math to measure out each clue. Then write the word from the Word List on page 46.

**Example:** the first 50% of *partly* + the middle 20% of *fractional* + the last 40% of *total* = <u>p</u> <u>a</u> <u>r</u> + <u>t</u> <u>i</u> + <u>a</u> <u>l</u> = ___________ partial

**1** the first 50% of *scarce* + the last 50% of *plenty* =

___ ___ ___ + ___ ___ ___ = ___________

**2** the first $1/2$ of *increase* + the last $5/11$ of *measurement* =

___ ___ ___ ___ + ___ ___ ___ ___ ___ ___ = ___________

**3** the first $1/6$ of *middle* + the middle $1/2$ of *mode* + the last $5/9$ of

*temperate* = ___ + ___ ___ + ___ ___ ___ ___ ___ = ___________

**4** the first $2/7$ of *destroy* + the middle 3 letters of *decimal* + the last $3/4$

of *fate* = ___ ___ + ___ ___ ___ + ___ ___ ___ = ___________

**5** the first 40% of *study* + the middle 50% of *data* + the last 25% of

*analysis* + the last 4 letters of *mathematics* = ___ ___ + ___ ___ +

___ ___ + ___ ___ ___ ___ = ___________

**Answer Yes or No**  Use what you know to answer **yes** or **no**.

___________ **6** Can you **monitor** an **odometer**?

___________ **7** If you have **copious** amounts of something, do you need to **ration** it?

___________ **8** Is it fair to **allocate** a **disproportionate** amount of dessert to some people?

___________ **9** Can a **partition** have **symmetry**?

___________ **10** Can **statistics** be used to **forecast** the weather?

**Speak It!**  Try out some of your new measurement vocabulary by talking about one of your favorite uses of measurement, such as sports statistics, local and world records, or ways in which you measure things in your home or classroom. Use as many of the vocabulary words from this unit as you can.

# Context Clues

*for Word Wisdom*

## The 1920s: Sounds of Change

**The period of the 1920s was a loud, wild, and crazy time in American history. With progress and prosperity seemingly everywhere, many people set out on a nearly decade-long party. Among the many things that characterized this party era were its sounds. It was a time for new music as well as new ways of playing and dancing to music.**

In 1926, the cover of *Life* magazine showed a saxophonist, a drummer, and a ukulele player. All were dancing as they played their instruments. Unlike a **subdued** classical musician, the drummer was creating the beat with one hand and tossing his drumstick into the air with the other. The ukulele player, a woman, was clad in a short dress and was strumming wildly. The third musician was bopping to the **peal** of the saxophone. Gaily dressed spectators exhibited their open-mouthed approval of the sounds that **resonated** through the packed room. With its bright red background, the cover illustrated the new, loud, fast-paced lifestyle. It was, after all, the 1920s, or, as it is often called, the Roaring Twenties.

What put all that loudness and roar in the Roaring Twenties? Technology helped. Advances in transportation and communications changed the economy and ways of life. Items like radios, cars, and refrigerators were beginning to be mass-produced so cheaply that more people could own them. People also had more free time and money than ever before. All these factors combined to make the economy hum and to give the impression of an unlimited and never-ending good life. It was as if the president had issued an **edict** that commanded, "Spend all your money!

Spend as much as you can, and then borrow to spend more!"

With more money, goods, and free time than ever before, people filled their lives with pleasure. They drove around in their new, fast cars and went to the movies. They blasted music on their newly acquired radios and played new albums on their **phonographs** that are unlike the small compact disc players of today. Music **blared** from dance halls, too. Jazz spread from its home in New Orleans to cities around the country, filling performance spaces with new and shocking **strains** and rhythms. A dance craze called the Charleston took the nation by storm. Its fast, leg-swinging movements and **raucous** sounds were completely unlike the accepted slower, quieter, and more tasteful dances of earlier eras.

Among those dancing were the flappers. These were the newly liberated women of the 1920s: women who were, for the first time, voting in the national elections. Some of these women were also working outside of their homes for the first time. Unlike the obedient and quiet women of earlier days, some flappers were **outspoken** and determined to change the world. Others were not so **vociferous** on the issues of the day. They were just young people in search of a good time.

# Context Clues Strategy

## Look for What the Word Is Contrasted With

**EXAMPLE:** The *boisterous* sports fans at the stadium, unlike the quiet neighborhood residents, did not hear the sirens.

**CLUE:** The phrase *unlike the quiet neighborhood residents* provides contrast with the boisterous fans. It tells what *boisterous* is "unlike."

Here are the steps for using this unit's context clues strategy to figure out the meaning of the word *phonograph*.

**Read** the sentence with the unknown word and some of the sentences around it.

*They blasted music on their newly acquired radios and played new albums on their **phonographs** that are unlike the small compact disc players of today.*

**Look** for context clues to the word's meaning. **What Is the Word Contrasted With?**

The sentence says that a phonograph was unlike small, compact disc players. If they aren't small and compact, they must be large.

**Think** about the context clues and other information you may already know.

I know that Edison invented the phonograph, so it's a pretty old invention for playing music. It makes sense that it is big and bulky. Phonographs are rarely used anymore.

**Predict** a meaning for the word.

A phonograph is probably a large type of record player.

**Check** a dictionary to be sure of the meaning.

*Phonograph* means "a record player."

# Unlock the Meanings

**Practice the Strategy**  Two of the boldfaced words from the essay about the 1920s on page 50 appear below. Use the context clues strategy on page 51 to figure out the meaning of each word.

## subdued

**Read** the sentence that uses the word *subdued* and some of the sentences around it.

**Look** for context clues to the word's meaning. **What Is the Word Contrasted With?**

__________________________________________

**Think** about the context clues. What other information do you know?

__________________________________________

**Predict** a meaning for the word *subdued*.

__________________________________________

**Check** your Word Wisdom Dictionary to be sure of the meaning for the word *subdued*. Which of the meanings for *subdued* fits the context?

__________________________________________

## outspoken

**Read** the sentence that uses the word *outspoken* and some of the sentences around it.

**Look** for context clues to the word's meaning. **What Is the Word Contrasted With?**

__________________________________________

**Think** about the context clues. What other information do you know?

__________________________________________

**Predict** a meaning for the word *outspoken*.

__________________________________________

**Check** your Word Wisdom Dictionary to be sure of the meaning for the word *outspoken*.

__________________________________________

✔ subdued
peal
resonate
edict
✔ phonograph
blare
strain
raucous
✔ outspoken
vociferous

**Use Context Clues**  You have been introduced to three vocabulary words from the essay on the 1920s. Those words are checked off in the Word List here. In the first column below, write the other seven words from the Word List. Use context clues to predict a meaning for each word in the second column. Then check the meanings in the Word Wisdom Dictionary. Write the definitions in the third column.

| | Vocabulary Word | Your Prediction | Dictionary Says |
| --- | --- | --- | --- |
| 1 | | | |
| 2 | | | |
| 3 | | | |
| 4 | | | |
| 5 | | | |
| 6 | | | |
| 7 | | | |

**WORD LIST**

- subdued
- peal
- resonate
- edict
- phonograph
- blare
- strain
- raucous
- outspoken
- vociferous

**Choose the Correct Word** Write the word from the Word List that completes each sentence. You may need to change the ending of the word. Underline any part of the sentence that helped you make your choice.

**1** The _________________ of bells could be heard at midnight.

**2** The beat of the big drum _________________ through the gymnasium and into the hall for several seconds.

**3** The national anthem _________________ from loudspeakers throughout the stadium.

**4** You can play that old record album on this antique _________________.

**5** The familiar _________________ of that old melody brought back a flood of memories.

**6** That _________________ sales associate was very insistent with her sales pitch.

**Find the Synonyms** Write the word from the Word List that is a synonym for the underlined word in each sentence.

**7** No one wanted to listen to the <u>harsh</u>, unpleasant music that Jared played.

_________________

**8** The <u>proclamation</u> was delivered when most of the townspeople were assembled. _________________

**9** Manuel seems <u>restrained</u> in front of adults, but he is the life of the party with his peers. _________________

**10** Kavita is a <u>free-speaking</u> supporter of recycling and conservation.

_________________

**Demonstrate Word Knowledge**   Use what you have learned about each boldfaced word to answer the questions or follow the directions.

**1** What is the difference between a **phonograph** and a **photograph**?

_______________________________________________

**2** Describe some **vociferous** behavior you have witnessed.

_______________________________________________

**3** Name something that **blares** in your home or school.

_______________________________________________

**4** Tell what you would do if you heard **raucous** sounds.

_______________________________________________

**5** Name a place where people are expected to behave in a **subdued** manner.

_______________________________________________

**Complete the Sentence**   Use what you have learned about the boldfaced word to complete each sentence.

**6** You might hear the **peal** of bells when _______________________

_______________________________________________

**7** One noise that **resonates** through the school sometimes is _______________

_______________________________________________

**8** I am **outspoken** when _______________________

_______________________________________________

**9** After floods or terrible storms, the governor might issue an **edict** saying _____

_______________________________________________

**10** You are likely to hear **strains** of music when walking near _______________

_______________________________________________

**Write It!**   Compare the music that you like to the music that your parents, or other adults you know, seem to like. Describe the two types of music. Use several of the words from the Part 1 Word List.

# PART 2

# Latin and Greek Roots

*for Word Wisdom*

## *Serious Sounds* by Lester Sutton: A Book Review

Here is a book review by Sandra Hill, a journalist for the local newspaper.

I heard so many people talking about *Serious Sounds* that I had to read it. Their opinions were so contradictory that I wondered whether I would like the book. I didn't.

The book jacket tells us that this is Lester Sutton's first book, but readers will realize that immediately. The story is about a teenage boy who does well in school, graduates at the top of his class, serves as class **valedictorian,** and then struggles to find his way in life. The boy is named José, and Sutton feels a need to provide the **phonetic** spelling of his name: *Ho-zay*. The **consonant** *j*, Sutton explains, is pronounced as *h*. Sutton must think little of his readers. He clearly does not realize how many millions of people speak Spanish—or at least know how to pronounce common Spanish names.

José, it seems, has a special skill in composing music. In fact, he writes a long sonata for a **symphony** while he is still in high school. The author describes this sonata as "flowing and **sonorous**, full of breathtaking combinations of sound." This description alone was almost enough to make me put down the book, but I kept plowing through it.

After high school, José enters a prestigious arts school and soon after attempts to compose a different kind of music. Unlike the sweetly flowing music he wrote in high school, this composition is full of **cacophony**. Instead of repeating measures and melodies, José fills his new work with **dissonance**. Not surprisingly, the reactions of José's instructors vary from amusement to boredom. Few of them are impressed, and José loses confidence in his skills. The unquestioning admiration and effortless success he experienced in high school are clearly in the past.

Determined to gain his instructors' respect, José composes a third sonata, this time relying on pleasing melodies and **assonance**. Both instructors and fellow students enthusiastically receive his work, and he is asked to present it at the school's annual public presentation. José is the youngest student ever invited to perform. You might have guessed that he receives a standing ovation.

As I read this mush, I wondered how much of it was autobiographical and how much was just wishful thinking on the author's part. The book jacket mentions that Sutton once played with a well-known symphony, but I wonder how long he lasted.

I strongly recommend that Sutton **abdicate** his role as a writer and return to music. Perhaps he has some skill in playing music, but he has none in combining subjects and **predicates**. Hopefully, his music allows him to communicate with others in a more meaningful way than his writing does.

**Practice the Context Clues Strategy** Here are two of the boldfaced words from the book review on page 56. Use the context clues strategy you learned in Part 1 on page 51 to figure out the meanings of these words.

## cacophony

**Read** the sentence that uses the word *cacophony* and some of the sentences around it.

**Look** for context clues to the word's meaning. Write down **What the Word Is Contrasted With**.

_________________________________________________

**Think** about the context clues. What other information do you know?

_________________________________________________

**Predict** a meaning for the word *cacophony*.

_________________________________________________

**Check** your Word Wisdom Dictionary to be sure of the meaning of the word *cacophony*. Write the definition here.

_________________________________________________

## dissonance

**Read** the sentence that uses the word *dissonance* and some of the sentences around it.

**Look** for context clues to the word's meaning. Write down **What the Word Is Contrasted With**.

_________________________________________________

**Think** about the context clues. What other information do you know?

_________________________________________________

**Predict** a meaning for the word *dissonance*.

_________________________________________________

**Check** your Word Wisdom Dictionary to be sure of the meaning of the word *dissonance*. Write the definition here.

_________________________________________________

# Unlock the Meanings

Many English words have Latin or Greek roots. Knowing the meanings of roots can help you understand the meanings of many words. Some of the words you studied in Part 1 have Latin or Greek roots. Each root below is related to speaking and sounds.

Latin Root: **dic, dict**
meaning: to say, to proclaim
English word: *edict*
meaning: a proclamation

Latin Root: **son**
meaning: sound
English word: *resonate*
meaning: to repeat, to echo

Greek Root: **phon**
meaning: sound
English word: *phonograph*
meaning: a record player

**WORD LIST**

valedictorian

phonetic

consonant

symphony

sonorous

cacophony

dissonance

assonance

abdicate

predicate

**Categorize by Roots**   Find these roots in the Word List. Write each word in alphabetical order in the correct column. Then circle the roots. Add other words you know that come from the same Latin or Greek roots.

Latin Root:
dic, dict

Latin Root:
son

Greek Root:
phon

Communication

| Prefix | Meaning | Example |
|--------|---------|---------|
| sym- | at the same time, together with | **sym-** (together) + **phon** (sound) + **y** = **symphony** |
| con- | against | |

**Use Roots and Prefixes**  Circle any roots and prefixes you find in the boldfaced words below. Use context clues, roots, and prefixes to write the meaning of the word. Use the Word Wisdom Dictionary to check your definitions.

**1** Andrew listened for the violins and flutes as the **symphony** played.

_______________________________________________

**2** According to the **phonetic** spelling in the dictionary, *ph* is often pronounced like an *f*.

_______________________________________________

**3** We covered our ears to shut out the **cacophony** coming from the wood shop.

_______________________________________________

**4** Because of public pressure to step down, the king will **abdicate**.

_______________________________________________

**5** The **valedictorian** gave a speech at the graduation ceremony.

_______________________________________________

**6** The two clarinets playing different tunes at once created **dissonance**.

_______________________________________________

**7** The **sonorous** voice of the opera singer held the audience spellbound.

_______________________________________________

**8** In a sentence, the **predicate** usually follows the subject.

_______________________________________________

**9** The poet used repeated long *o* and long *e* sounds to create **assonance**.

_______________________________________________

**10** The name Meg begins and ends with a **consonant**.

_______________________________________________

# Process the Meanings

**WORD LIST**

- valedictorian
- phonetic
- consonant
- symphony
- sonorous
- cacophony
- dissonance
- assonance
- abdicate
- predicate

**Choose the Correct Word**  Write the word in parentheses that completes each sentence. Underline any part of the sentence that helped you make your choice.

**1** Sometimes people have trouble hearing the difference between the ________________________ *p* and *b*. (consonants; phonetics)

**2** A complete sentence needs a subject and a ________________________. (consonant; predicate)

**3** We all congratulated the ________________________ on her accomplishments and her speech. (cacophony; valedictorian)

**4** If some members of the band play the wrong notes, the ________________________ it causes will be most unpleasant. (dissonance; symphony)

**5** "High in the sky" is an example of ________________________. (assonance; predicate)

**6** The ________________________ sounds of the waterfowl drifted across the lake at sundown. (predicate; sonorous)

**7** The ________________________ performed the music of Beethoven and Handel in the new concert hall. (valedictorian; symphony)

**8** The ________________________ caused by the loud sirens, the marching band, and the cheering crowd frightened my dog. (assonance; cacophony)

**9** No one expected the queen to ________________________ her throne and leave the country. (abdicate; predicate)

**10** The ________________________ alphabet helped Eduardo learn how to say English words. (phonetic; sonorous)

**Complete the Sentence**   Use what you have learned about the boldfaced word to complete each sentence.

**1** I enjoyed the performance by the **symphony** because _______________________

________________________________________________________________

**2** Tra-la-la is an example of **assonance** because ________________________

________________________________________________________________

**3** At the concert, I found Mr. Davidson's **sonorous** tone _________________

________________________________________________________________

**4** I used the **phonetic** alphabet to __________________________________

________________________________________________________________

**5** The leader of the troubled nation will **abdicate** because _______________

________________________________________________________________

**Solve the Riddle**   Write a word from the Word List on page 60 for each clue. You will need to change the ending of one word.

**6** They combine with vowels to make words. ___________________________

**7** It goes with a subject to make a sentence. __________________________

**8** A student with "all A's" might be this. ___________________________

**9** It goes with clanging, banging, blaring, and booming.

_________________________

**10** If musicians don't play together and create unpleasant sounds, this is what

you get. ________________________

**Speak It!**   Compare and contrast a place or experience that is soothing to your ears with one that is not. Use as many of the words from the Part 2 Word List as you can.

# PART 3 Reference Skills

*for Word Wisdom*

## Standing Up:
# Saying "No!"

**One vital communication skill is difficult for people of all ages to master, and that is the ability to say "no" when you need or want to refuse a request.**

Too many of us become involved in activities that are unhealthy, boring, expensive, or pointless because we don't want to hurt the other person's feelings or because the other person just won't stop asking.

How many times have you wished you could **retract** your agreement to do something with a friend? You should have replied to the request with one **succinct** word—no! Instead, you offered a long, rambling reply, but even all those words did not clearly communicate your lack of interest in or time for the suggested activity.

How can you say "no" and not end up in a stressful debate? First, simply say, "No, thanks." **Reiterate** this phrase as many times as necessary, repeating it until the walls **reverberate** with "No, thanks." Stand by your answer.

Perhaps the other person is not willing to give up and **retorts,** "Why not?" If the request is against your values and goals, such as someone asking you to cheat on a test or smoke a cigarette, you don't have to explain your refusal. You don't need to **placate** someone who is determined to bully you into doing something you don't want to do. A firm, **terse** "No, thanks" is enough to explain your position.

Maybe the other person still keeps **exhorting** you to join him or her in the activity. This is a good time to turn the situation around and ask your own questions. For example, you might ask, "Why would you want me to do that?" or "What would happen if we did that?" These questions will encourage the other person to think about the consequences of an unwise or ill-advised activity.

Some requests may threaten your health, your reputation, or your peace of mind. When you refuse them, you must appear confident, not **reticent**. Remember that your goals and values are just as important to you as the other person's goals are to him or her. You have no reason to agree to an activity that does not suit you for some reason. Stand up for yourself!

Other times, the request might be reasonable, but you might be unable to grant it. Then you might explain the reason, such as making previous plans or having a big project due the next day. You don't need to **expound** on your reason—or get into a debate. You should explain your reason confidently, without apologizing for having other things to do.

Saying "no" is uncomfortable at times, even for adults. Sometimes it seems easier to go along with the other person rather than getting into an argument or hurting his or her feelings. However, you have the right to control your life and not let friends take over. When your parents are making the request, well, that's an entirely different situation!

**Practice the Context Clues Strategy**   Here are two of the boldfaced words from the selection on page 62. Use the context clues strategy you learned in Part 1 on page 51 to figure out the meanings of these words.

## succinct

**Read** the sentence that uses the word *succinct* and some of the sentences around it.

**Look** for context clues to the word's meaning. Write down **What the Word Is Contrasted With.**

_________________________________________________

**Think** about the context clues. What other information do you know?

_________________________________________________

**Predict** a meaning for the word *succinct*.

_________________________________________________

**Check** your Word Wisdom Dictionary to be sure of the meaning of the word *succinct*. Write the definition here.

_________________________________________________

## reticent

**Read** the sentence that uses the word *reticent* and some of the sentences around it.

**Look** for context clues to the word's meaning. Write down **What the Word Is Contrasted With.**

_________________________________________________

**Think** about the context clues. What other information do you know?

_________________________________________________

**Predict** a meaning for the word *reticent*.

_________________________________________________

**Check** your Word Wisdom Dictionary to be sure of the meaning of the word *reticent*. Write the definition here.

_________________________________________________

**Looking Up Base Words** Most dictionaries do not have a separate entry for every form of a word. If a word ends with a common suffix, you usually have to find it by looking up the **base word,** the word without any suffixes.

For example, if you wanted to look up the word *abdicated* or *abdicating,* you would find it under the entry for *abdicate.* If you wanted to find the word *symphonies,* you would need to look up the word *symphony.*

**Use a Dictionary** Look up the following words in a dictionary. Write the other forms of the word the dictionary gives.

**1** expound ______________________________________________

**2** retract ______________________________________________

**3** terse ______________________________________________

**4** retort ______________________________________________

**5** reiterate ______________________________________________

**Find the Base Words** Write the entry word you would look for to find these words.

**6** succinctness ______________________________

**7** reticently ______________________________

**8** reverberating ______________________________

**9** placated ______________________________

**10** exhorts ______________________________

**Find the Meaning**

1. Use context clues.
2. Look for a familiar root, prefix, or suffix.
3. If the context or a word part doesn't help, check the dictionary.

**Define the Words** Follow the steps above to decide on the meaning of each boldfaced word. Write the meaning of the word. Then write 1, 2, or 3 to show which steps you used.

**WORD LIST**

retract

succinct

reiterate

reverberate

retort

placate

terse

exhort

reticent

expound

**1** Sound **reverberates** through the empty hall.

_______________________________________________

**2** When I realized my words were hurtful, I wanted to **retract** my statement.

_______________________________________________

**3** Her answer consisted of one **succinct** word: "no."

_______________________________________________

**4** The professor **expounded** for several hours on his research.

_______________________________________________

**5** Liz was **reticent** about saying unkind things about others.

_______________________________________________

**6** When I asked the child to stop, I did not expect his sassy **retort**.

_______________________________________________

**7** Our teacher **exhorted** us to work harder if we expected to pass the tests.

_______________________________________________

**8** I tried to **placate** my crying sister by giving her a toy.

_______________________________________________

**9** The teacher did not wish to **reiterate** instructions she had already given.

_______________________________________________

**10** The angry woman gave a **terse** reply to the reporter's question.

_______________________________________________

# Process the Meanings



**Find the Antonyms** Write the word from the Word List that is an antonym of the boldfaced word or words. You may need to change the ending of the word.

**1** Leah is usually very **boisterous** when she is at my house.

______________________

**2** When we performed in that empty room, the sounds **were absorbed**.

______________________

**3** People often commented on Jeffrey's **roundabout** methods of stating his ideas. ____________________

**4** Are those forms designed to **frustrate** applicants after they have waited in long lines? ____________________

**5** The explanation would have been better if it had not been so **lengthy**.

______________________

**Classify the Words** Add the correct vocabulary word or words to each group.

**6** take back, withdraw, ____________________

**7** explain, interpret, ____________________

**8** urge, encourage strongly, ____________________

**9** reply, comeback, ____________________

**10** repeat, restate, ____________________

**11** quiet, shy, ____________________

**12** echo, resound, ____________________

**13** soothe, pacify, ____________________

**14** concise, brief, ____________________

# Apply What You've Learned

**Demonstrate Word Knowledge**  Use what you have learned about each boldfaced word to answer the questions or follow the directions.

**1** Write a **succinct** answer to the question "Where do you live?"

**2** What would cause a newspaper to **retract** a story?

**3** What sounds seem to **reverberate** around your house, apartment, or neighborhood?

**4** Write a **terse** reply to the question "How are you today?"

**5** Offer a **retort** to this command: "Clean up your room!"

**6** Explain how you might **placate** a friend who is upset with you.

**7** Name some advice that you think is worth **reiterating**.

**8** Name a situation in which you would **exhort** a friend to be careful.

**9** Name a topic you could **expound** on for a long time.

**10** Name a situation in which you've felt **reticent**.

**Write It!**  Write a dialogue between someone who is angry and someone who is trying to calm that person down. Use several words from the Part 3 Word List.

PART **4**

# Review

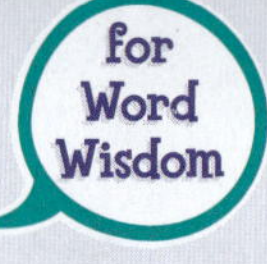



**Categorize by Part of Speech** Study the Word List. Write each word in the correct column of the chart. Some words have multiple meanings and can go in more than one column.

## WORD LIST

- subdued
- peal
- resonate
- edict
- phonograph
- blare
- strain
- raucous
- outspoken
- vociferous
- valedictorian
- phonetic
- consonant
- symphony
- sonorous
- cacophony
- dissonance
- assonance
- abdicate
- predicate
- retract
- succinct
- reiterate
- reverberate
- retort
- placate
- terse
- exhort
- reticent
- expound

| Noun | Verb | Adjective |
|------|------|-----------|
|      |      |           |

**Choose the Correct Word** Write the vocabulary word in parentheses that completes each sentence.

**1** New laws and taxes were announced in the king's ________________. (edict; retort)

**2** Dan likes to ________________ on the importance of safety on the school bus. (abdicate; expound)

**3** When those trumpets ________________, it is difficult to hear the flutes. (blare; retract)

**4** Some words double a final ________________ when suffixes are added to them. (predicate; consonant)

**5** The principal could not be heard above the ________________ of pots and pans in the cafeteria. (peal; cacophony)

**Classify the Words** Write the vocabulary word that belongs in each group.

**6** subject, direct object, prepositional phrase, ________________

**7** rock band, jazz quartet, choir, ________________

**8** master of ceremonies, keynote speaker, spokesperson, ________________

**9** radio, CD player, record player, ________________

**10** reply, response, answer, ________________

**11** loud, harsh, disagreeable, ________________

**12** outspoken, loudmouthed, insistent, ________________

**13** disharmony, conflict, disagreement, ________________

**14** recall, take back, withdraw, ________________

**15** abandon, resign, surrender, ________________

# Taking Vocabulary Tests

## TEST-TAKING STRATEGY

Many tests are scored by machine. For this reason, neatness counts. When you fill in a circle that contains a letter, be sure to darken it completely. If you change your mind and erase your first choice, be sure to erase it completely. Finally, avoid making stray marks in other parts of the test. You do not want the machine to misread any correct answers!

### Sample:

Fill in the letter of the item that most nearly means the OPPOSITE of the boldfaced word.

**retract**

Ⓐ restate
Ⓑ put forward
Ⓒ repeat
Ⓓ take back

**Practice Test**  Fill in the letter of the item that most nearly means the OPPOSITE of the boldfaced word.

**1 terse**
Ⓐ tense
Ⓑ lengthy
Ⓒ symphonic
Ⓓ lively

**2 raucous**
Ⓐ fast
Ⓑ long-lasting
Ⓒ difficult
Ⓓ soothing

**3 succinct**
Ⓐ vague
Ⓑ soft-spoken
Ⓒ vocal
Ⓓ sassy

**4 reticent**
Ⓐ reserved
Ⓑ shrill
Ⓒ aggressive
Ⓓ shy

**5 outspoken**
Ⓐ restrained
Ⓑ argumentative
Ⓒ echoed
Ⓓ funny

**6 subdued**
Ⓐ pealing
Ⓑ phonetic
Ⓒ uncommunicative
Ⓓ noisy

**7 placate**
Ⓐ exhort
Ⓑ annoy
Ⓒ please
Ⓓ retort

**8 dissonance**
Ⓐ communication
Ⓑ recital
Ⓒ harmony
Ⓓ conflict

**9 sonorous**
Ⓐ loud
Ⓑ repetitive
Ⓒ sleepy
Ⓓ plain

**10 vociferous**
Ⓐ concise
Ⓑ melodic
Ⓒ quiet
Ⓓ off-key

**Build New Words**

**Use Suffixes** The suffixes *-ation, -tion,* and *-ion* can be added to some verbs to make them nouns. Use these suffixes to make new words from *abdicate, exhort, reverberate, retract,* and *reiterate.* You will need to change some spellings. Write a sentence using each new word.

| Word | + Suffix | = New Word | Sentence |
|---|---|---|---|
| abdicate | | | |
| exhort | | | |
| reverberate | | | |
| retract | | | |
| reiterate | | | |

**Speak It!** What musical performances, lectures, parades, school assemblies, or other performances have you attended lately? Choose one to describe or evaluate. Use as many vocabulary words from this unit as you can to tell about what you heard, how it all sounded, and what you did or didn't like about it.

# Context Clues



## A Force for Change:
# Sojourner Truth

The history of the United States may be seen as an ongoing march toward justice for all. Although the words of the Declaration of Independence and the Constitution guarantee equality, over the years our society has faced many problems. In the 1800s, Sojourner Truth made it her mission to address the problems of her time and help change our world.

Her name was Isabella Bomefree; she was also known as Isabella Van Wagener. Born a slave, she was **prohibited** from learning to read or write. Even without those skills, she became one of the most famous people ever to work for social justice and **reform** in America. Today she is remembered by the name she chose for herself—Sojourner Truth.

Truth chose her name because she wanted to be known as a woman who carried the truth to others. Her life consisted of **sojourns,** brief or temporary stays between her journeys.

Although Truth had been owned by several masters, she was able, over time, to **transcend** the life of slavery. When her youngest child was sold, she took matters into her own hands by having local Quakers help her gain her son's return. She also obtained her own freedom in 1827. Once she was on her own, she began to **fraternize** with people who opened her eyes to new religious and social ideas. She wanted to influence people on a number of issues, including social justice.

Today, Sojourner Truth is remembered as an **abolitionist,** a person who worked to abolish slavery. She became involved in the antislavery movement in the 1840s. She appeared before audiences as a representative of African Americans. Her ability to move and sway her audience became well known, and she gained a reputation as a powerful orator. She also dictated and published *The Narrative of Sojourner Truth,* one of the many books used in the argument for the **emancipation** of slaves from their bondage.

Sojourner Truth is also remembered as a **feminist,** a person who supports women's rights. Truth is known for a speech she gave at a women's rights conference in Akron, Ohio, in 1851. The conference had been taken over by men who did not want equal rights for women. They believed women were not smart enough. Truth got up and delivered her "Ain't I a Woman?" speech, which showed that she was as tough and as able as any man.

Throughout her life, Truth worked tirelessly for justice and equality. During the Civil War, she helped **fugitive** slaves who escaped to the North, and she also helped soldiers. After the war, she ministered to the needs of **displaced** people driven from their homes. In Washington, she met personally with President Lincoln. She also submitted a plan to Congress for assigning government lands in the West to newly freed people.

# Context Clues Strategy

## Look for Definitions, Descriptions, or Synonyms

**EXAMPLE:** In college, Anton decided to major in *sociology, the study of human society*.

**CLUE:** The phrase *the study of human society* tells what *sociology* is. In fact, those words define *sociology*.

Here are the steps for using this context clues strategy to figure out the meaning of the word *abolitionist*.

**Read** the sentence with the unknown word and some of the sentences around it.

*Today, Sojourner Truth is remembered as an **abolitionist**, a person who worked to abolish slavery. She became involved in the antislavery movement in the 1840s.*

**Look** for context clues to the word's meaning. What **Definitions, Descriptions, or Synonyms** do you find?

The first sentence says that an abolitionist is a person who wanted to abolish slavery.

**Think** about the context clues and other information you may already know.

I know that *abolish* means "end forever." The word *abolitionist* is similar to *abolish*. I know that many people wanted to end slavery, and they were willing to go to war to make sure that happened.

**Predict** a meaning for the word.

An abolitionist is "a person who believes in, and fights for, ending slavery."

**Check** your Word Wisdom Dictionary to be sure of the meaning.

The word *abolitionist* means "a person who works to end a law or custom."

**Practice the Strategy**  Two of the boldfaced words from the essay on page 72 appear below. Use the context clues strategy on page 73 to figure out the meaning of each word.

### sojourns

📖 **Read** the sentence that uses the word *sojourns* and some of the sentences around it.

🔍 **Look** for context clues to the word's meaning. What **Definitions, Descriptions,** or **Synonyms** can you find?

_______________________________________________

💡 **Think** about the context clues. What other helpful information do you know?

_______________________________________________

➡️ **Predict** a meaning for the word *sojourns*.

_______________________________________________

✔️ **Check** your Word Wisdom Dictionary to be sure of the meaning of the word *sojourn*.

_______________________________________________

### feminist

📖 **Read** the sentence that uses the word *feminist* and some of the sentences around it.

🔍 **Look** for context clues to the word's meaning. What **Definitions, Descriptions,** or **Synonyms** can you find?

_______________________________________________

💡 **Think** about the context clues. What other helpful information do you know?

_______________________________________________

➡️ **Predict** a meaning for the word *feminist*.

_______________________________________________

✔️ **Check** your Word Wisdom Dictionary to be sure of the meaning of the word *feminist*.

_______________________________________________

**Use Context Clues** The three words from the essay that you have already learned have a check mark by them. In the first column, write the remaining seven words from the Word List. In the second column, predict a meaning for each word using context clues. Then look up each word in your Word Wisdom Dictionary, and write its definition in the third column.

**WORD LIST**

prohibit
reform
✔ sojourn
transcend
fraternize
✔ abolitionist
emancipation
✔ feminist
fugitive
displaced

| Vocabulary Word | Your Prediction | Dictionary Says |
| --- | --- | --- |
| 1 | | |
| 2 | | |
| 3 | | |
| 4 | | |
| 5 | | |
| 6 | | |
| 7 | | |

**WORD LIST**

- prohibit
- reform
- sojourn
- transcend
- fraternize
- abolitionist
- emancipation
- feminist
- fugitive
- displaced

**Choose the Definitions** Choose the correct definition for each word from the Word List. Write the definition on the line.

**1** emancipation ________________________________

act of freeing          freedom in the United States

**2** fugitive ________________________________

person who supports equal rights     person who escapes

**3** sojourn ________________________________

interrupted travel         brief stopover during travel

**4** fraternize ________________________________

socialize in a friendly way     socialize in harmful ways

**5** displaced ________________________________

moved because of good planning     forced to move

**6** feminist ________________________________

supports women's rights     works for women's charities

**7** abolitionist ________________________________

works to end slavery     works for many different reforms

**8** transcend ________________________________

go forward         go beyond

**9** prohibit ________________________________

forbid a behavior        encourage a behavior

**10** reform ________________________________

social issue        social change

# Apply What You've Learned

**Find the Synonyms** Write the word from the Word List that is a synonym for each underlined word.

**1** All the television stations are broadcasting information about the <u>escapee</u>.

_______________________________

**2** Marcie worked for <u>change</u> in the city laws to require more recycling.

_______________________________

**3** Many people had discussed the <u>freeing</u> of slaves before the war began.

_______________________________

**4** Our <u>stopover</u> at that town will be just for one night.

_______________________________

**5** The new law will <u>forbid</u> people from using cell phones while driving.

_______________________________

**Use the Words Correctly in Writing** Rewrite each sentence in your own words. Use the word in parentheses in your sentence.

**6** Frederick Douglass spent many years working to end slavery. (abolitionist)

_____________________________________________________

**7** Many people were forced from their homes during the flood. (displaced)

_____________________________________________________

**8** Leah voted for the candidate who supported women's rights. (feminist)

_____________________________________________________

**9** Roberto spends time getting to know his neighbors. (fraternizing)

_____________________________________________________

**10** Mariella and Sam worked to rise above their differences. (transcend)

_____________________________________________________

**Write It!** Write one or two paragraphs to describe a change you would like to see in the way society treats young people. Use words from the Word List on page 76.

# PART 2

# Latin Roots

*for Word Wisdom*

## Fraternal Groups:
# To Join or Not to Join?

**Do you plan to attend college some day? If so, you probably have many questions. Which college would be best for you? What should you study? After you get to college, how can you make new friends?**

Your parents and guidance counselors can help you choose a college and a major. After you are on campus and want to find new friends, you might consider joining a **fraternity** (a group for men) or a sorority (a group for women). These groups serve as a family away from home. Often new members are assigned to a "big brother" or "big sister." This person helps them adjust to college and become more comfortable there.

Many fraternities and sororities have their own houses where members can **cohabit**. Sometimes a group lives in a wing of a college dormitory. In this way, members get to know each other very well. Houses often have written rules to **formalize** each person's rights and responsibilities. These rules help each **inhabitant** know what is expected of him or her so everyone can live together peacefully.

Fraternities and sororities also provide social activities that can make it easier to meet other students on campus. The more people you meet, the more likely you are to find others who share your interests and values. Many of these social activities are relaxed and informal, while others might require a certain kind of clothing.

Your big brother or sister can tell you about the **formality** of each event and the activities involved in it. You do not have to **conform,** or do what everyone else is doing. At least you will know what is expected.

Of course, fraternities and sororities are not just social groups. Many members participate in programs to help others in the college and in the community. For example, members might volunteer in hospitals, tutor young people after school, or clean up parks. Some help build or **rehabilitate** houses for people with low incomes. Others raise money for charities or important causes. A group might also publicize a community issue or problem that needs to be addressed.

Fraternities and sororities encourage their members to work hard in their college classes. Members cannot let their grades fall below a certain level if they want to stay in the group. Group interactions also help members learn social skills that will continue to benefit them after they graduate from college. These groups promote strong values by providing positive role models and encouraging **inhibitions** on negative behavior. In addition, **fraternal** groups elect officers, offering opportunities for members to strengthen their leadership skills.

You may think of yourself as a **nonconformist** who would be uncomfortable in a fraternity or sorority. While that may be true, be sure to explore the advantages of joining such a group before deciding it is not for you.

**Practice the Context Clues Strategy**  Here are two of the boldfaced words from the essay on page 78. Use the context clues strategy you learned in Part I on page 73 to figure out the meanings of these words.

### fraternity

**Read** the sentence that uses the word *fraternity* and some of the sentences around it.

**Look** for context clues to the word's meaning. What **Definitions, Descriptions, or Synonyms** can you find?

_______________________________________________

**Think** about the context clues. What other information do you know?

_______________________________________________

**Predict** a meaning for the word *fraternity*.

_______________________________________________

**Check** your Word Wisdom Dictionary to be sure of the meaning of the word *fraternity*. Write the definition here.

_______________________________________________

### conform

**Read** the sentence that uses the word *conform* and some of the sentences around it.

**Look** for context clues to the word's meaning. What **Definitions, Descriptions, or Synonyms** can you find?

_______________________________________________

**Think** about the context clues and other information you already know.

_______________________________________________

**Predict** a meaning for the word *conform*.

_______________________________________________

**Check** your Word Wisdom Dictionary to be sure of the meaning of the word *conform*. Write the definition here.

_______________________________________________

Many English words have Latin roots. Knowing the meanings of roots can help you understand the meanings of many words. Many of the words you studied in Part 1 have Latin roots. All the words are related to society.

Latin Root: **frat**
meaning: brother
English word: *fraternize*
meaning: to socialize with someone

Latin Root: **hab, hib**
meaning: to have, suitable
English word: *prohibit*
meaning: to prevent

Latin Root: **form**
meaning: shape
English word: *reform*
meaning: a change for the better

**Categorize by Roots**  Find these roots in the words in the Word List. Write each word in alphabetical order in the correct column. Then circle the roots you find. Think of other words you know that have the same root. Write them in the correct column.

**WORD LIST**

fraternity

cohabit

formalize

inhabitant

formality

conform

rehabilitate

inhibition

fraternal

nonconformist

## Society

Latin Root:
**frat**

Latin Root:
**hab, hib**

Latin Root:
**form**

___________   ___________   ___________

___________   ___________   ___________

___________   ___________   ___________

___________   ___________   ___________

| Prefix | Meaning |
| --- | --- |
| re- | again |
| non- | not |
| in- | in |



**re-** (again) + **form** (shape) = **reform**

**Use Roots and Prefixes** For each boldfaced word, circle the root and any prefix you find. Use roots, prefixes, and context clues to write the meaning of each boldfaced word. Use your Word Wisdom Dictionary to check your definitions.

**1** Did buffalo and deer **cohabit** in the same areas of the western states?

_______________________________________________

**2** Carla's **inhibitions** kept her from asking the star for an autograph.

_______________________________________________

**3** That **fraternity** raises money each year to help local volunteer fire fighters.

_______________________________________________

**4** Aaron, a **nonconformist**, refused to wear the same styles his friends wear.

_______________________________________________

**5** They are brothers, but the boys do not have a **fraternal** resemblance.

_______________________________________________

**6** Our society hopes to **rehabilitate** criminals to make them better citizens.

_______________________________________________

**7** We wrote down the new rules in order to **formalize** them.

_______________________________________________

**8** The **inhabitants** of that facility must be at least sixty-five years old.

_______________________________________________

**9** All players had to **conform** to the rules of the team.

_______________________________________________

**10** The **formality** of the occasion required Amanda to wear a ball gown.

_______________________________________________

**WORD LIST**

- fraternity
- cohabit
- formalize
- inhabitant
- formality
- conform
- rehabilitate
- inhibition
- fraternal
- nonconformist

**Use the Words Correctly in Writing** Rewrite each sentence in your own words using the word in parentheses in your sentence.

**1** The physical therapy will help Jake regain full use of his left leg. (rehabilitate)

_______________________________________________

**2** Some people don't rebel, but rather act according to society's standards. (conform)

_______________________________________________

**3** In every situation, Kenesha does things her own way. (nonconformist)

_______________________________________________

**4** The fire did not affect people living in Buildings C and D. (inhabitants)

_______________________________________________

**5** Jenna had the job but had to be interviewed anyway. (formality)

_______________________________________________

**Choose the Correct Word** Write the word from the Word List that completes each sentence. You will need to add an ending to one word. Underline any part of the sentence that helped you make your choice.

**6** Jeremy shared similar interests with Marcus and the other members of his

_______________________________ .

**7** Zach wanted to dance, but his _______________________________ held him back.

**8** Business people _______________________________ agreements when they sign

contracts.

**9** Frank has a close, _______________________________ friendship with Rodrigo.

**10** Do all those animals peacefully _______________________________ the

same area?

# Apply What You've Learned

**Link to Your Life**  Write sentences to follow the directions below.

**1** Name some interests that might serve as a base of a **fraternity**.

_______________________________________________

**2** Name two animals that **cohabit** in a local park or forest.

_______________________________________________

**3** Describe a time when you had to act in a certain way for the sake of **formality**.

_______________________________________________

**4** Name a **fraternal** organization you have read or heard about.

_______________________________________________

**5** Explain how you might **formalize** an agreement with a friend.

_______________________________________________

**6** Name a way in which society tries to **rehabilitate** people in prison.

_______________________________________________

**Solve the Riddles**  Write a word from the Word List to solve each riddle.

**7** I march to the beat of a different drummer. _______________________

**8** I can keep you from acting on an impulse. _______________________

**9** I am found in a house or an environment. _______________________

**10** I command, "Act like others do." _______________________

**Speak It!** Research the life of someone who was able to overcome difficulties or injuries and then made an important contribution to society. Give an oral report on that person. Use as many words from the Word List on page 82 as you can when making your report.

# Reference Skills

*for Word Wisdom*

## Brown vs. Board of Education:
## Separate but Equal?

**Imagine being kept away from your best friends simply because of the color of your skin. At one time, this was the reality. In fact, until the mid-1950s, black people and white people lived separately throughout much of the United States.**

Daily life in some parts of America was different before you and your parents were born—white people and black people were kept separate. They could not sit together in restaurants, in movie theaters, or on buses. They had to use different drinking fountains and restrooms. Often, black customers were required to enter stores through a back door. They rode in the back of the bus. Most importantly, black and white children in many communities did not go to the same schools. Instead, each group attended schools that were supposedly "separate but equal."

**Segregation,** a policy keeping members of different races apart, had long been the rule in many schools. However, in 1951, Oliver Brown, a black father living in Kansas, did not want his daughter to walk to a school that was a mile from their home. But the school board refused to let her go to a closer school. That school was reserved for white children. At the time, the National Association for the Advancement of Colored People (NAACP) was the **predominant** group fighting for civil rights. When Mr. Brown asked the NAACP for help, the group took the case to court.

Unconcerned, the Kansas school board members felt total **solidarity**. They fully intended to maintain the current **status** of their schools. They believed that separate schools prepared children for the segregation they would face later in life. By attending separate schools, they would learn the appropriate **decorum,** or behavior, for their adult lives.

In 1952, the case reached the U.S. Supreme Court. In 1896, that court had decided that "separate but equal" facilities were acceptable. This ruling made school segregation legal. In 1952, however, lawyer Thurgood Marshall represented the NAACP. He argued that separate schools taught black children that they were inferior to white children. In 1954, the Supreme Court finally ruled that separate schools were not equal. It ordered schools across the nation to end segregation.

Many white people resisted desegregation. Rioting occurred in some cities. Nevertheless, black people were encouraged in their struggle for equality. The NAACP and **affiliate** groups, along with leaders from other **ethnic** groups, fought for the Civil Rights Act of 1964 and the Voting Rights Act of 1965. Finally, African Americans could no longer be **patronized** as second-class citizens who had to learn to accept discrimination.

In 1967, Thurgood Marshall was sworn in as the first African American Supreme Court justice. He became **privy** to confidential information and helped make decisions that have shaped our nation. His life is **inseparable** from the fight for equality and civil rights. That fight continues today.

### segregation

**Read** the sentence that uses the word *segregation* and some of the sentences around it.

**Look** for context clues to the word's meaning. What **Definitions, Descriptions, or Synonyms** can you find?

_______________________________________________

**Think** about the context clues. What other information do you know?

_______________________________________________

**Predict** a meaning for the word *segregation*.

_______________________________________________

**Check** your Word Wisdom Dictionary to be sure of the meaning of the word *segregation*. Write the definition here.

_______________________________________________

### decorum

**Read** the sentence that uses the word *decorum* and some of the sentences around it.

**Look** for context clues to the word's meaning. What **Definitions, Descriptions, or Synonyms** can you find?

_______________________________________________

**Think** about the context clues and other information you already know.

_______________________________________________

**Predict** a meaning for the word *decorum*.

_______________________________________________

**Check** your Word Wisdom Dictionary to be sure of the meaning of the word *decorum*. Write the definition here.

_______________________________________________

## Internet Skills: Choosing Search Terms

To research a topic on the Internet, use a search engine and type in the right **search terms**. Having good vocabulary skills can help you find what you want on the Internet.

Follow these guidelines for getting information on the Internet.
1. Use **specific search terms**. For example, if you want to research emancipation in the United States, you need to eliminate other types of emancipation. To be specific, enter: *emancipation U.S.*
2. Put **quotation marks** around terms that you want to appear together. For example, to research the Civil War, use quotation marks, and enter: *"Civil War"*
3. Add words that will **narrow your search**; for example, enter: *segregation South buses restaurants "public places"*

**Edit the Search Terms**   Each of the following computer search topics uses a word from the Word List on page 87. Rewrite each search entry to make it more specific or useful. You may need to use a dictionary to look up some terms.

**1** the war in Bosnia and the region's history of ethnic hatred

_________________________________________________

**2** the success of the labor movement called Solidarity in Poland, led by Lech Walesa

_________________________________________________

**3** status of women in American society around 1900

_________________________________________________

**4** Emily Post rules of decorum for weddings

_________________________________________________

**5** hospitals that are affiliated with Harvard University

_________________________________________________

**Find the Meaning**

1. Use context clues.
2. Look for a familiar root, prefix, or suffix.
3. If the context or a word part doesn't help, check the dictionary.



**Define the Words**  Follow the steps above to decide on the meaning of each boldfaced word. Write the meaning of the word. Then write 1, 2, or 3 to show which steps you used to decide on the meaning.

**1** During the war, the whole country felt **solidarity** with the other nations on its side.

_______________________________________________

**2** There are many themes in that novel, but love of family is **predominant**.

_______________________________________________

**3** Dr. Oliveira's sense of **decorum** made him attend the ceremony in a tuxedo.

_______________________________________________

**4** The paper company is an **affiliate** of a multinational corporation.

_______________________________________________

**5** His job in the guidance office makes Steve **privy** to confidential information.

_______________________________________________

**6** During the years of **segregation**, the two neighbors attended different schools.

_______________________________________________

**7** Alexei is proud of his **ethnic** roots in Bulgaria.

_______________________________________________

**8** Claudia does not like being **patronized** just because she is young.

_______________________________________________

**9** Because of the **status** of his visa, he couldn't work in the United States.

_______________________________________________

**10** The best friends were **inseparable**; they did everything together!

_______________________________________________

**WORD LIST**

segregation

predominant

solidarity

status

decorum

affiliate

ethnic

patronize

privy

inseparable

**Choose the Correct Word** Write the word from the Word List that completes each sentence. You may need to add an ending to some words.

**1** Mei Ling felt a strong sense of _________________ with her field hockey team.

**2** That business is a(n) _________________ of the Lopez Sisters Construction Company.

**3** What is the _________________ of your application for the job as a lifeguard?

**4** In the 1950s, some people favored integration while others wanted _________________.

**5** My neighbor Sheyda has taught me some of the important _________________ traditions of Iran.

**6** At first, only a few doctors were _________________ to the information about the rare disease.

**7** Many believe that physical and emotional well-being are so connected, they are _________________.

**8** Do patients feel they're being _________________ by being called "honey"?

**9** Talking on the cell phone is not appropriate _________________ during a wedding.

**10** Fair pay was the _________________ concern of the labor group.

**Classify the Words** Add the correct word from the Word List to each group.

**11** oneness, togetherness, _________________

**12** secret, private, _________________

**13** most central, most important, _________________

**14** place, honor, _________________

**15** sponsor, support, _________________

# Apply What You've Learned

**Use the Rhyming Clues** Write a word from the Word List that is suggested by each clue.

**1** how it is now ________________________

**2** important one, second to none ________________________

**3** act with tact ________________________

**4** set apart from the start ________________________

**5** seem sweet but still mistreat ________________________

**6** together forever ________________________

**7** association in relation ________________________

**8** trace by place or race ________________________

**9** aim as a group; never betray the troop ________________________

**10** so in the know (it's a secret, though!) ________________________

**Choose Antonyms** Circle the word that is an antonym for each vocabulary word.

**11** segregation      isolation, integration

**12** predominant      major, minor

**13** affiliate      enemy, associate

**14** inseparable      joined, disconnected

**15** decorum      chaos, etiquette

**Write It!** Make a list of rules for getting along with others. Use as many words from the Word List on page 88 as you can.

# Review

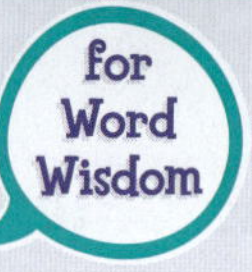


**Categorize the Words** Write the words from the Word List in the correct sections below. You will not use all of the words. Some words belong in more than one group.

## WORD LIST

- prohibit
- reform
- sojourn
- transcend
- fraternize
- abolitionist
- emancipation
- feminist
- fugitive
- displaced
- fraternity
- cohabit
- formalize
- inhabitant
- formality
- conform
- rehabilitate
- inhibition
- fraternal
- nonconformist
- segregation
- predominant
- solidarity
- status
- decorum
- affiliate
- ethnic
- patronize
- privy
- inseparable

**Words That Name People**

_______________________

_______________________

_______________________

_______________________

_______________________

**Words That Name Actions Performed by People**

_______________________

_______________________

_______________________

_______________________

_______________________

_______________________

**Words That Can Describe People**

_______________________

_______________________

_______________________

_______________________

**Positive Goals Achieved by People**

_______________________

_______________________

**Choose the Correct Word**  Write the word from the Word List that completes each sentence in the paragraph. You will need to change the endings of two words.

When the hurricane was first predicted, people immediately began evacuating their homes. These **1** _________________ people needed space in shelters. Luckily, the Red Cross and several of its **2** _________________ were already on the scene. They had **3** _________________ procedures for providing emergency help. Their **4** _________________ concern was to meet people's basic needs for food and shelter. The Red Cross workers also kept people advised of the **5** _________________ of the approaching storm.

**Write the Sentences**  Write a sentence that uses all of the words in each group. You may use the words in any order. You may also change the endings of words.

**6** Maddie, sojourn, Seattle

_______________________________________________

**7** Ryan, fraternity, band

_______________________________________________

**8** Adam, formality, occasion

_______________________________________________

**9** Darius, end, segregation

_______________________________________________

**10** dogs, cats, cohabit

_______________________________________________

# Taking Vocabulary Tests

## TEST-TAKING STRATEGY

When you are asked to find synonyms, be careful! There may be more than one answer choice that is a synonym or a near synonym. Be sure to read every answer choice so that you select the answer that is closest in meaning to the test word.

**Sample:**

Fill in the circle of the word or words that have the SAME or ALMOST THE SAME meaning as the boldfaced word in each phrase.

the new **reforms**

- ○ laws
- ○ activists
- ○ social events
- ● social changes

**Practice Test**  Fill in the circle of the word or words that have the SAME or ALMOST THE SAME meaning as the boldfaced word in each phrase.

**1** the feeling of **solidarity**
- ○ social consciousness
- ○ respect
- ○ disbelief
- ○ unity

**2** **ethnic** pride
- ○ normal
- ○ cultural
- ○ original
- ○ situational

**3** **fraternal** feelings
- ○ brotherly
- ○ joyful
- ○ organizational
- ○ regretful

**4** **fugitive** from justice
- ○ nonconformist
- ○ person on the run
- ○ misfit
- ○ prisoner

**5** **decorum** for the occasion
- ○ intentions
- ○ religious feelings
- ○ proper behavior
- ○ contributions

**6** the recent **inhabitant**
- ○ relationship
- ○ enterprise
- ○ buyer
- ○ resident

**7** **prohibit** the practice
- ○ demand
- ○ grant
- ○ forbid
- ○ question

**8** the necessary **sojourn**
- ○ business trip
- ○ temporary stay
- ○ vacation
- ○ long journey

**9** the wedding **formalities**
- ○ rules or customs
- ○ courses
- ○ relationships
- ○ associations

**10** tendency to **patronize**
- ○ purchase
- ○ retreat
- ○ look down upon
- ○ overlook

# Play with Language

**Solve a Crossword Puzzle** Write words from the Word List on page 90 to complete the crossword puzzle.

## Across

**3** in on a secret

**6** restraint on behavior

**7** occupant

**8** organization related to another institution

**10** interact with socially

## Down

**1** type of reformer

**2** to visit often, as in a restaurant

**3** standing out in a group

**4** live in the same area with

**5** bring back to a former state or condition

**9** related to culture, race, or religion

**Speak It!** Play the role of a social reformer. Give a speech in which you attempt to persuade your listeners about a social issue. Use as many words from the Word List on page 90 as you can.

# PART 1

# Context Clues



## Get Up and Go:
# The Benefits of Exercise

**Today, about half of all adults in the U.S. are overweight. This rate has doubled in the last twenty years. Bad eating habits are one major cause of this alarming trend. A second major cause is our inactive way of life. Read this essay to find out how and why you should get moving.**

Do you spend hours in front of a computer, at a desk, or in front of the TV? If you do, it's likely that you are too **sedentary**. Health professionals would offer you this advice: Get up and go.

No matter how old you are, there are numerous reasons to put an end to laziness or **inertia** and to start exercising on a regular basis. Exercise lowers blood pressure. It makes you less likely to develop heart disease, stroke, and diabetes. Exercise strengthens your bones, joints, and muscles. It improves your mood and, in some cases, helps cure depression. If all those reasons aren't enough to get you moving, consider this: People who exercise **convert** fewer calories into fat than people who sit still. In combination with proper diet, exercise can help you lose weight or stay at the recommended weight. **Lethargy** is fine for the places where you must be seated, like a train or a bus. At other times, get moving!

You might think that to start a meaningful exercise program you need **access** to a gym, sports facility, or other specialized location. You might also think that you have to purchase fancy exercise equipment. That is simply not true.

Another misconception you might have is that you cannot do moderate or easy exercise but must do something **strenuous** instead. Again, nothing could be further from the truth. Research has shown that when people don't exercise, any amount of increased activity is beneficial to their health.

Exercising regularly is important. Try to set up a reasonable, workable schedule for yourself. Keep to your schedule and don't **deviate** from it. Once you establish the rhythm of exercise, it will be easier. Some researchers recommend exercising every day for the first twenty-one days while you are trying to establish a new exercising way of life. Once you are in the habit of exercise, they say, you will have created a **momentum** that will be difficult to break. In fact, you will probably feel low or weak if you have to miss your exercise sessions! On the other hand, once you get in the rhythm, exercise can **energize** and motivate you. Like many runners and other fitness lovers, you may feel more **dynamic** and full of life as a result of your exercise. There are many reasons to stop sitting still. For your health and well-being, get up, get going, and stay on the move.



Movement

UNIT 5

# Context Clues Strategy

## Look for the Location or Setting

**EXAMPLE:** Traffic is *sluggish* on the narrow city streets during rush hour.

**CLUE:** This sentence gives a setting that includes the place and the time: *the narrow city streets during rush hour*. Because rush hour is busy and narrow city streets allow only a few cars to pass at a time, the context helps the reader understand that *sluggish* means "slow."

Using context clues means studying all the words in the sentence in which an unfamiliar word appears. It also means looking for additional clues in the sentences that precede and follow the unfamiliar word. Here are the steps to figure out the meaning of the word *sedentary*, which appears in the essay about exercise.

**Read** the sentence with the unknown word and some of the sentences around it.

*Do you spend hours in front of a computer, at a desk, or in front of the TV? If you do, it's likely that you are too **sedentary**.*

**Look** for context clues to the word's meaning. What clues to the word's **Location or Setting** do you find?

The first sentence names three locations or settings: *in front of a computer, at a desk, in front of the TV.*

**Think** about the context clues and other information you already know.

I know that all the locations named are places to sit. When people are sitting in those places, they don't move very much.

**Predict** a meaning for the word.

*Sedentary* must mean "doing too much sitting."

**Check** the Word Wisdom Dictionary to be sure of the meaning.

The word *sedentary* means "sitting most of the time; not moving."

**Practice the Strategy**   Look at the two words from the essay on page 94. Use the context clues strategy on page 95 to figure out the meaning of each word.

## lethargy

📖 **Read** the sentence that uses the word *lethargy* and some of the sentences around it.

🔍 **Look** for context clues to the word's meaning. What clues to the word's **Location or Setting** can you find?

_______________________________________________

💡 **Think** about the context clues. What other information do you know?

_______________________________________________

➡️ **Predict** a meaning for the word *lethargy*.

_______________________________________________

✔️ **Check** your Word Wisdom Dictionary to be sure of the meaning for the word *lethargy*. Write the definition here.

_______________________________________________

## access

📖 **Read** the sentence that uses the word *access* and some of the sentences around it.

🔍 **Look** for context clues to the word's meaning. What clues to the word's **Location or Setting** can you find?

_______________________________________________

💡 **Think** about the context clues. What other helpful information do you know?

_______________________________________________

➡️ **Predict** a meaning for the word *access*.

_______________________________________________

✔️ **Check** your dictionary to be sure of the meaning for the word *access*. Decide which of the meanings in the dictionary fits the context.

_______________________________________________

**Use Context Clues**  The three vocabulary words that you have learned so far are checked off in the Word List. Write the other seven words from the Word List. Use context clues to write a possible meaning for each word under "Your Prediction." Then check the meanings in the Word Wisdom Dictionary. Write the definition under "Dictionary Says."

| | Vocabulary Word | Your Prediction | Dictionary Says |
|---|---|---|---|
| 1 | | | |
| 2 | | | |
| 3 | | | |
| 4 | | | |
| 5 | | | |
| 6 | | | |
| 7 | | | |

**WORD LIST**

- sedentary
- inertia
- convert
- lethargy
- access
- strenuous
- deviate
- momentum
- energize
- dynamic

**Use the Words Correctly in Writing**   Rewrite each sentence in your own words. Use the word in parentheses in your sentence. You may need to add an ending to the word.

**1** Molly's parents were worried by her lack of energy. (lethargy)

_______________________________________

**2** Although Eduardo seems shy, he is a forceful public speaker. (dynamic)

_______________________________________

**3** Lee hit the ball so hard that its force carried it over the fence. (momentum)

_______________________________________

_______________________________________

**4** Once we got the overloaded wagon moving, it was easy to push it along. (inertia)

_______________________________________

_______________________________________

**5** Rosa's workout at the gym filled her with energy for the rest of the afternoon. (energize)

_______________________________________

_______________________________________

**Classify the Words**   Add the correct word from the Word List to each group.

**6** change into, turn into, _______________________________

**7** stray, turn away, _______________________________

**8** difficult, physically demanding, _______________________________

**9** entrance, right of way, _______________________________

**10** seated, stationary, _______________________________

# Apply What You've Learned

**Complete the Sentences**   Complete each sentence below.

**1** I think of Felipe as a **dynamic** person because __________________

__________________________________________________

**2** Sharlene is a **sedentary** person who __________________________

__________________________________________________

**3** When water boils, it **converts** a liquid into ___________________

__________________________________________________

**4** Some things that **energize** me are ___________________________

__________________________________________________

**5** Kayla got **access** to the locked building because ________________

__________________________________________________

**Connect the Words**   Write a word from the list to answer each question.

**6** Which word goes with "It's a back-breaking job"?

__________________________________________________

**7** Which word goes with "I don't feel like doing anything today; go ahead

without me"? _______________________________________

**8** Which word goes with "Let's take a different path this time"?

__________________________________________________

**9** Which word goes with "When a cart is moving, it likes to keep moving"?

__________________________________________________

**10** Which word goes with "When a cart is stopped, it's hard to get it going

again"? ___________________________________________

**Write It!**   A puppy's activity level is usually higher than that of an old dog's activity level. Contrast the behavior of a puppy and an old dog. Use some words from the Part 1 Word List.

# Latin Roots

*for Word Wisdom*

## Erosion:
# Beaches on the Move

**Have you ever wanted to live on a beach? You might imagine having a small house at the water's edge so that you could just walk out the door and dip your toes in the waves. But building a house within reach of ocean waves is a foolish venture. The waves will soon make it clear that Mother Nature is still in charge.**

Coastal erosion is expensive because of the land lost and the costly attempts to stop that loss. The Federal Emergency Management Agency (FEMA) estimates that erosion will cost $500 million annually if people keep flocking to our shores and erosion trends continue.

As each wave breaks on the shore, it loosens grains of sand. As the wave **recedes** into the ocean, it carries away at least some of that sand. The **incessant** waves, pounding the shore day and night, can carry off tons of sand. The strength and speed of the waves, along with the direction of the current, help determine how much erosion occurs. Longshore currents, for example, **traverse** the shoreline. They run parallel to the shore and carry sand farther down the beach.

Many communities and individual homeowners try to **intercede** in this process. For example, some have built wooden or rock seawalls to **divert** the force of the waves away from the sand. Nevertheless, studies have shown that these structures may actually increase erosion nearby. The washing away of sand just does not **cease**.

Communities have also shipped in truckloads of sand as part of beach nourishment programs. However, this sand is soon **conveyed** out to sea by the **wayward** waves. Still, the United States government spends as much as $150 million a year on beach nourishment. State and local governments and homeowners, hoping to stop their beaches from disappearing, spend even more.

Beaches are changing, ever-evolving forms as waves not only remove sand, but also deposit it. What waves remove one week or one season, they might replace at some point in the future. However, this does not help people who attempt to build too close to the water. Their structures cannot remain suspended in space until the sand **reverts** to its original location—if it ever does. Instead, when enough of their foundations wash away, the houses collapse into the water.

Researchers are trying to learn more about the patterns of erosion and wave circulation. However, it is too expensive to send an **envoy** to stand at the water's edge indefinitely and monitor the loss of sand. Instead, a program at The Ohio State University uses a video camera to tape the wave patterns. It tracks the movement of foam created by the breaking waves to determine how the water is flowing near the shore.

Regardless of our efforts, erosion will remain a ceaseless, powerful force of nature that will continue as long as Earth spins.

**Practice the Context Clues Strategy**  Here are two of the boldfaced words from the essay on page 100. Use the context clues strategy you learned in Part 1 on page 95 to figure out the meanings of these words.

## incessant

**Read** the sentence that uses the word *incessant* and some of the sentences around it.

**Look** for context clues to the word's meaning. What clues to the word's **Location or Setting** can you find?

_______________________________________________

**Think** about the context clues and other information you already know.

_______________________________________________

**Predict** a meaning for the word *incessant*.

_______________________________________________

**Check** your Word Wisdom Dictionary to be sure of the meaning of the word *incessant*. Write the definition here.

_______________________________________________

## traverse

**Read** the sentence that uses the word *traverse* and some of the sentences around it.

**Look** for context clues to the word's meaning. What clues to the word's **Location or Setting** can you find?

_______________________________________________

**Think** about the context clues and other information you already know.

_______________________________________________

**Predict** a meaning for the word *traverse*.

_______________________________________________

**Check** your Word Wisdom Dictionary to be sure of the meaning of the word *traverse*. Write the definition here.

_______________________________________________

Many English words have Latin roots. Knowing the meanings of roots can help you understand the meanings of many words. Many of the words you studied in Part 1 have Latin roots. Each root below is related to movement.

Latin Root: **ced, ces, ceas**
meaning: go, lead, yield
English word: *access*
meaning: the right to enter or use

Latin Root: **vers, vert**
meaning: turn
English word: *convert*
meaning: to change into another form

Latin Root: **via, vey, voy**
meaning: way or road
English word: *deviate*
meaning: to turn aside or away from

## WORD LIST

- recede
- incessant
- traverse
- intercede
- divert
- cease
- convey
- wayward
- revert
- envoy

**Categorize by Roots**   Find these roots in the Word List. Write each word in alphabetical order in the correct column. Circle the roots you find. There is one word that isn't spelled like *via* but comes from the root *via*. Then add other words with these roots that relate to movement.

Latin Root: ced, ces, ceas

Latin Root: vers, vert

Latin Root: via, vey, voy

________  ________  ________

________  ________  ________

________  ________  ________

________  ________  ________

________  ________  ________

**Movement**

| Prefix | Meaning | Example |
|--------|---------|---------|
| re- | back | **re-** (back) + **ced** (to go) + **e** = **recede** |
| inter- | between | |
| in- | not | |

**Use Roots and Prefixes**   Circle the root and any prefix you find in the boldfaced words. Use context clues, roots, and prefixes to write the meaning of the word. Check your definitions in the Word Wisdom Dictionary.

**1** After the flood, did the water **recede** to normal levels?

_______________________________________________

**2** The king sent his **envoy** to meet with the townspeople.

_______________________________________________

**3** The **wayward** child did not obey her parents and acted on impulse.

_______________________________________________

**4** The dog's **incessant** barking kept us awake all night.

_______________________________________________

**5** The lift will **convey** the skiers to the top of the mountain.

_______________________________________________

**6** When I made a mistake, my dad had to **intercede** for me.

_______________________________________________

**7** I hoped the baby would **cease** crying so that I could study.

_______________________________________________

**8** If the new strategies don't work, we'll **revert** to our old methods.

_______________________________________________

**9** It took several days for the expedition to **traverse** the mountains.

_______________________________________________

**10** The engineers tried to **divert** the flow of the river to prevent flooding.

_______________________________________________

**WORD LIST**

recede
incessant
traverse
intercede
divert
cease
convey
wayward
revert
envoy

**Use the Words Correctly in Writing**  Rewrite each sentence in your own words. Use the word in parentheses.

**1** The store will close down all operations at midnight tonight. (cease)

_______________________________________________

**2** Jorge had a reputation for being smart but disobedient. (wayward)

_______________________________________________

**3** A helicopter will take the injured motorist to a hospital in the city. (convey)

_______________________________________________

**4** The climbers had to cross the slippery ridge in the storm. (traverse)

_______________________________________________

**5** We were kept awake by the whirring noise all night. (incessant)

_______________________________________________

**Choose the Correct Word**  Write the word from the Word List that best completes each sentence. You may need to change the ending of the word. Underline any part of the sentence that helped you make your choice.

**6** Although Grandpa will be sixty soon, his hairline has not

_______________________________ .

**7** When the computers are down, the library _______________________ to the old-fashioned ways of processing books.

**8** One thief _______________________ our attention while the other one grabbed Lilly's purse!

**9** The diplomatic _______________________ from Peru carried a request to the president of Mexico.

**10** To stop the argument between the two neighbors, the police had to

_______________________________ .

**Complete the Analogies**  Write the word that best completes each analogy.

**1** Stop : start :: **cease** : ______________________.
  a. begin         c. end
  b. turn          d. delay

**2** Unyielding : inflexible :: **incessant** : ______________________.
  a. disturbing    c. nonstop
  b. changeable    d. giving

**3** Cowardly : brave :: **wayward** : ______________________.
  a. unruly       c. beautiful
  b. dangerous   d. obedient

**4** Backward : forward :: **recede** : ______________________.
  a. stop         c. proceed
  b. change     d. shout

**5** Doctor : physician :: **envoy** : ______________________.
  a. teacher     c. musician
  b. messenger  d. politician

**Answer the Questions**  Answer each question below.

**6** Why might you **intercede** in an argument?

____________________________________________

**7** How would you **convey** a stack of firewood to your house?

____________________________________________

**8** How might you **divert** attention away from yourself?

____________________________________________

**9** When might you **revert** to a slower or more difficult way of doing things?

____________________________________________

**10** How might you **traverse** a narrow stream?

____________________________________________

**Speak It!**  Do some research and give an oral report on one or more famous explorers like Lewis and Clark or Richard Byrd. Use as many words as you can from the Part 2 Word List.

# PART 3 Reference Skills

*for Word Wisdom*

## People-Watching:
## People on the Move

**Have you ever been in a shopping mall and observed the different ways that people interact with each other and their surroundings? The variety is amazing.**

Here comes a boy who is about 14, **meandering** past the stores, casually glancing at the items displayed in the windows. Hair artfully arranged, dressed in the latest clothes, he is clearly here to be seen, not to shop. As he **saunters** past, we can see his eyes dart about, checking to see who is admiring him. Pretending to notice no one, he probably could describe every person around him in considerable detail, especially those of the young female variety.

Behind him, a harried young mother, loaded down with a diaper bag and two bags from mall stores, struggles with two preschoolers. Her young son **capers** ahead of her, singing to himself and dancing around slower walkers. Her daughter, slightly older and much more sophisticated, **dawdles** at each window, examining its contents with interest until her mother pulls her along. A few stores in front of them, someone has dropped an ice-cream cone on the floor. As the family approaches it, the mother urges her children to **tread** carefully around the mess, but the younger one, accidentally or on purpose, **traipses** right through it. Now he leaves chocolate footprints behind him. His sister rolls her eyes and shakes her head at his lack of social graces.

Not far behind them, a gray-haired couple skillfully skirts the ice cream. They **promenade** arm in arm, perhaps as part of their daily exercise program. Content with themselves, they occasionally glance at each other and smile. After all these years, no conversation is necessary.

A young woman in sweats effortlessly **lopes** around the couple, pumping her arms. On this blustery, wintry day, perhaps she is making the mall part of her exercise program, too. After all, you don't have to expose yourself to a biting wind to stretch those calf muscles.

Not everyone in the mall is on the move, of course. On a wooden bench across the wide hallway sits a man with ragged clothing and an unshaved face. Still, he is not begging for handouts. Instead, this **vagabond** seems to be merely resting before continuing the day's journeys. As you watch out of the corner of your eye, he rises from the bench and **hobbles** away, perhaps drawn by the aroma of the coffee shop down the way. He pulls some change out of his pants pocket as he limps away. He continues to just wander around the mall. Maybe he is simply a man with his own dress code.

People-watching reminds us of our different interests, motivations, and situations. The mall offers not just a place to shop, but a place to observe and better appreciate each other.

### dawdles

**Read** the sentence that uses the word *dawdles* and some of the sentences around it.

**Look** for context clues to the word's meaning. What clues to the **Location or Setting** can you find?

_______________________________________________

**Think** about the context clues and other information you already know.

_______________________________________________

**Predict** a meaning for the word *dawdle*.

_______________________________________________

**Check** your Word Wisdom Dictionary to be sure of the meaning of the word *dawdle*. Write the definition here.

_______________________________________________

### vagabond

**Read** the sentence that uses the word *vagabond* and some of the sentences around it.

**Look** for context clues to the word's meaning. What clues to the **Location or Setting** can you find?

_______________________________________________

**Think** about the context clues and other information you already know.

_______________________________________________

**Predict** a meaning for the word *vagabond*.

_______________________________________________

**Check** your Word Wisdom Dictionary to be sure of the meaning of the word *vagabond*. Write the definition here.

_______________________________________________

**Dictionary Skills: Parts of Speech**   Dictionaries provide many types of information about words, including the word's part of speech. In many cases, a word can be more than one part of speech. These parts of speech can appear in the same definition, as well as in different entries for the same word. In the following entries, each part of speech (*n., v.*) is abbreviated and appears in italic type before each definition.

**ca•per**[1] /kā′ pər/ *n.* **1.** a playful hop. *Bill's caper showed his pleasure.* **2.** a prank. *The caper wasn't completely harmless, because it upset Mrs. Levy.* **3.** a plan for a crime. *The caper involved breaking and entering.*

**ca•per**[2] /kā′ pər/ *n.* **1.** flower bud of a shrub that is pickled and used to add flavor to food. *Some cooks use lemons and capers to season chicken.* **2.** the shrub that bears capers. *The caper is a Mediterranean shrub.*

**ca•per**[3] /kā′ pər/ *v.* **ca•pered, ca•per•ing, ca•pers.** to leap or jump around playfully. *The happy children caper on the playground.*

**Write the Parts of Speech**   Look up the following Part 3 Movement words in a dictionary. List all the parts of speech the dictionary gives for each.

1 tread   _______________________________________________

2 meander   _______________________________________________

3 vagabond   _______________________________________________

4 dawdle   _______________________________________________

5 traipse   _______________________________________________

6 hobble   _______________________________________________

7 lope   _______________________________________________

8 saunter   _______________________________________________

9 promenade   _______________________________________________

10 caper   _______________________________________________

**Find the Meaning**

1. Use context clues.
2. Look for a familiar root, prefix, or suffix.
3. If the context or a word part doesn't help, check the dictionary.



**Define the Words**  Follow the steps above to write the meaning of each boldfaced word. Then write 1, 2, or 3 to show which steps you used.

**1** I believe that we have **tread** this path through the woods many times.

_______________________________________________

**2** With her long legs, Emma **loped** effortlessly across the field.

_______________________________________________

**3** The train will leave in five minutes, so we don't have time to **dawdle**.

_______________________________________________

**4** On that beautiful spring day, Ali and I **traipsed** all over the neighborhood.

_______________________________________________

**5** Without buying anything, Jill **meandered** around the stores to pass the time.

_______________________________________________

**6** Tom acted as if he had all the time in the world as he **sauntered** toward us.

_______________________________________________

**7** Being always on the move, Willy the **vagabond** had no permanent address.

_______________________________________________

**8** I didn't know Lei hurt her leg until I saw her **hobble** down the street.

_______________________________________________

**9** In the days before the automobile, couples used to **promenade** along the waterfront.

_______________________________________________

**10** Mrs. Sanchez smiled as she watched her daughter twirl and **caper** in the playroom.

_______________________________________________

# Process the Meanings



meander

saunter

caper

dawdle

tread

traipse

promenade

lope

vagabond

hobble

**Select the Answers**  Read each question below. Underline the best answer.

**1** Who would be most likely to **hobble**?
a. a tired runner
b. an injured runner
c. a runner at the starting line

**2** Why might you **saunter**?
a. You have an urgent message to deliver.
b. You are in pain.
c. You have time on your hands.

**3** Where would you most likely **traipse**?
a. around the park
b. across the dance floor to the sounds of a band
c. down the aisle at a wedding

**4** Why might you **dawdle**?
a. because you lost track of time
b. to catch up with your friends
c. to increase your heart rate

**5** Who would be most likely to **promenade**?
a. a businessperson on the way to a meeting
b. a father getting his three children off to school
c. a couple with a new baby in the park

**6** Which of these animals might **lope**?
a. a horse
b. a snake
c. a hawk or an eagle

**Classify the Words**  Add the correct word from the Word List to each group.

**7** step, trample, ______________________________

**8** wanderer, drifter, ______________________________

**9** leap, jump, ______________________________

**10** wander, move about aimlessly, ______________________________

**Find Examples** Each vocabulary word is followed by two sentences. One sentence is an example of the word. Write **E** next to the Example.

**1** lope

________ You dash across the finish line just in time.

________ You easily cross the finish line with no runners in sight.

**2** caper

________ With a look of glee, you dance and twirl across the room.

________ With a look of determination, you dash across the room.

**3** vagabond

________ A man goes to a different campground every night.

________ A man checks into a hotel for vacation.

**4** tread

________ You hear the sound of footsteps moving down the hall.

________ You hear the sound of people bumping into each other.

**5** meander

________ The couple casually window-shops in the mall for hours.

________ The couple walks straight into the store and buys a gift.

**6** saunter

________ Erica approaches Mari eagerly to give her the news.

________ Erica takes her time approaching Mari with some gossip.

**7** traipse

________ You walk all around the large amusement park.

________ You spend the day on one ride at the amusement park.

**8** promenade ________ You move slowly down the sidewalk, enjoying yourself.

________ You walk with a heavy step down the sidewalk.

**9** dawdle

________ The children have their picnic and clean up quickly.

________ The children take a long time to finish their picnic.

**10** hobble

________ The soldier makes his way, somehow, to the emergency station.

________ The soldier runs swiftly to the emergency station.

**Write It!** Write a paragraph for a visitor's guide to a great city you have visited or would like to visit. Name some activities visitors and their children can enjoy there. Use several of the vocabulary words from the Part 3 Word List.

# Review



## WORD LIST

- sedentary
- inertia
- convert
- lethargy
- access
- strenuous
- deviate
- momentum
- energize
- dynamic
- recede
- incessant
- traverse
- intercede
- divert
- cease
- convey
- wayward
- revert
- envoy
- meander
- saunter
- caper
- dawdle
- tread
- traipse
- promenade
- lope
- vagabond
- hobble

**Complete the Continuum** Study each set of words below.
Arrange each word on the continuum from **inactive** to **active**.

**Inactive**　　　　　　　　　　　　　　　**Active**

inertia, lope, saunter

1 ————————— 2 ————————— 3 —————————▶

dynamic, meander, lethargy

4 ————————— 5 ————————— 6 —————————▶

traipse, caper, hobble, sedentary

7 ———— 8 ———— 9 ———— 10 ————▶

**Categorize by Connotation** Decide if each word in the box below
has a negative or positive connotation. Then write the word in the correct
column.

| dawdle | energize | promenade | vagabond | wayward | intercede |

**Positive Connotation**　　　　　　　**Negative Connotation**

______________________________

______________________________

______________________________

**Check the Meanings**  Read each sentence and decide if the boldfaced word is used correctly. Write **C** for Correct or **I** for Incorrect.

**1** Is the town planning to **divert** that forest? ______

**2** How did early settlers **traverse** those rapids? ______

**3** I need your help soon, so please don't **dawdle**! ______

**4** Let's **meander** to Tim's house quickly after school. ______

**5** Those dogs **traipse** around this field as if they own it! ______

**Choose the Correct Word**  Complete each sentence by choosing the correct word in parentheses. You will need to change the ending of a word.

**6** Ms. Sereno had to _____________________ (intercede, convey) when

the customers got into an argument.

**7** Curtis could not shake his feelings of _____________________.

(lethargy, momentum)

**8** Although Sean is a grown man, he sometimes _____________________

(recede, revert) to calling his mother "Mommy."

**9** No one knows how the hackers got _____________________ (access,

tread) to Carla's computer files.

**10** The children's _____________________ (inertia, incessant) questions

showed their excitement.

**Identify the Relationships**  Read each pair of words. Write **S** if they are Synonyms and **A** if they are Antonyms.

**11** energized, dynamic ______

**12** inertia, momentum ______

**13** incessant, continual ______

**14** deviate, conform ______

**15** strenuous, relaxing ______

# Taking Vocabulary Tests

## TEST-TAKING STRATEGY

Are you nervous when you take tests? That's normal—but almost never helpful. Before starting a test, take a deep breath and tell yourself to relax. Remember the strategies you have learned that will help you do well. Then trust yourself to work calmly, carefully, and thoughtfully. This will allow you to concentrate on the task.

**Sample:**

Fill in the circle of the item that means the SAME or NEARLY THE SAME as the boldfaced word.

**sedentary**
- O stretched
- O traipse
- ● seated
- O jogging

**Practice Test** Fill in the circle of the item that means the SAME or NEARLY THE SAME as the boldfaced word.

**1 traverse**
- O complete quickly
- O move quietly
- O reverse
- O travel across

**2 incessant**
- O irregular
- O casual
- O tiring
- O constant

**3 envoy**
- O representative
- O soldier
- O traveler
- O aviator

**4 convey**
- O carry
- O change around
- O stretch
- O travel together

**5 tread**
- O skip
- O walk
- O weave
- O limp

**6 convert**
- O change
- O use up
- O move rapidly
- O retreat

**7 deviate**
- O move slowly
- O backtrack
- O turn aside
- O speed up

**8 wayward**
- O strong
- O effortless
- O disobedient
- O delayed

**9 cease**
- O pant
- O stop
- O grab
- O train

**10 caper**
- O move ahead
- O hesitate
- O leap playfully
- O stroll aimlessly

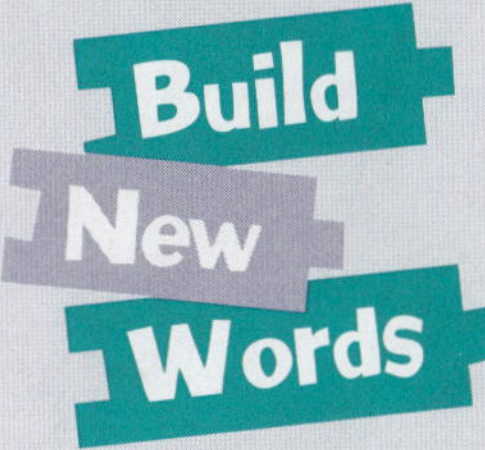


**Change Verbs to Nouns** Adding the *-ion* suffix to a verb will usually change the verb into a noun. However, sometimes adding the *-ion* suffix requires you to change the spelling of the word. Note how the spellings change when the *-ion* suffix is added to these words:

| Verb | + -ion | = Noun |
|---|---|---|
| provide | -ion | provision |
| revolt | -ion | revolution |
| emit | -ion | emission |

Add the *-ion* suffix to these verbs from this unit to make them nouns. Check your spellings in the Word Wisdom Dictionary.

| Verb | + -ion | = Noun |
|---|---|---|
| **1** revert | -ion | __________ |
| **2** divert | -ion | __________ |
| **3** convert | -ion | __________ |
| **4** recede | -ion | __________ |
| **5** intercede | -ion | __________ |

**Speak It!** Perform a radio broadcast of an imaginary news story, theatrical performance, or sporting event. When you finish, let the class discuss your broadcast. Use as many words from this unit as you can.

# Context Clues

for Word Wisdom

## Fairy Tales: Good and Evil Fight It Out Forever

**Humans share a love of stories. Fairy tales are among the most commonly told stories. Still, have you ever stopped to consider what they really say? Read this article to find out about the battle between good and evil in fairy tales.**

Everyone has read, heard, or seen fairy tales. Fairy tales are stories about impossible events in unreal times and places. Their theme is good **versus** evil. Usually the battle between these two opposites is short, and it almost always ends up in a satisfying way. There is nothing **ambiguous** about the outcome of a fairy tale. Instead, the resulting happiness (or occasional doom) is clear and certain.

A fairy tale might begin when the protagonist, or main character, breaks a law or commits some kind of **transgression**. One consequence might be the character's **banishment,** or sending away. Another might be the assignment of some kind of task that will undo the evil. Very often, this task involves overcoming a great obstacle or a terrible villain.

Villains take various forms in fairy tales. They can be witches, wizards, trolls, gnomes, or giants. Gnomes are tiny while giants are huge, but both are equally evil. Trolls, who are also **vile** creatures of varying sizes, live in caves, in the hills, or under bridges. Although all these villains are nasty antagonists, the hero or heroine is usually **implacable** in the face of them. He or she fights a good fight with a grim and unstoppable determination.

Fairy tales also include fairies, genies, kind witches, and other guardians who come to the rescue of the hero or heroine. In sharp contrast to the **reprehensible** villains, these helpers and givers are always good.

Fairy tales are immensely popular and widespread. People who study folklore have found more than 500 variations of the Cinderella story and more than 400 versions of Snow White! One reason for the popularity of fairy tales is the soothing world view they often present. For example, the character who is honest and good often finds happiness at the end. Often the poor become rich. The **ethical** person, rather than the immoral one, triumphs. Those who have done evil are **thwarted** or punished. These hopeful messages satisfied the earliest people who told the tales, and they still satisfy us today.

Although the first oral fairy tales are now thousands of years old, new tales and retellings appear constantly. These retellings help ensure that the optimistic and **affirmative** fairy tale lives happily ever after.

Good and Bad

UNIT 6

# Context Clues Strategy

## Look for Antonyms

**EXAMPLE:** Those two brothers are just the opposite: one is stingy and the other is truly *magnanimous*.

**CLUE:** This sentence sets up a contrast by telling you that two people are opposite. Because one is described as stingy, it is easy to infer that *magnanimous* means just the opposite, or "generous."

Using the context is a good way to understand the meaning of a new word. Here are the steps for using this context clues strategy to figure out the meaning of the word *ambiguous* from the article about fairy tales.

**Read** the sentence with the unknown word and some of the sentences around it.

*There is nothing **ambiguous** about the outcome of a fairy tale. Instead, the resulting happiness (or occasional doom) is clear and certain.*

**Look** for context clues to the word's meaning. What **Antonyms** do you find?

The first sentence says the outcome of a fairy tale is not ambiguous. The second sentence says the outcomes are "clear and certain." The word *instead* signals a clue.

**Think** about the context clues and other information you may already know.

I know the opposite of *clear and certain* is *unclear and uncertain*.

**Predict** a meaning for the word *ambiguous*.

*Ambiguous* probably means "unclear."

**Check** your Word Wisdom Dictionary to be sure of the meaning.

*Ambiguous* means "unclear."

**Practice the Strategy**  Look at the two words from the essay on page 116. Use the context clues strategy on page 117 to figure out the meaning of each word.

## reprehensible

**Read** the sentence that uses the word *reprehensible* and some of the sentences around it.

**Look** for context clues to the word's meaning. What **Antonyms** can you find?

_______________________________________________

**Think** about the context clues. What other helpful information do you know?

_______________________________________________

**Predict** a meaning for the word *reprehensible*.

_______________________________________________

**Check** a dictionary to be sure of the meaning for the word *reprehensible*. Write the dictionary meaning.

_______________________________________________

## ethical

**Read** the sentence that uses the word *ethical* and some of the sentences around it.

**Look** for context clues to the word's meaning. What **Antonyms** can you find?

_______________________________________________

**Think** about the context clues. What other helpful information do you know?

_______________________________________________

**Predict** a meaning for the word *ethical*.

_______________________________________________

**Check** a dictionary to be sure of the meaning for the word *ethical*. Write the dictionary meaning.

_______________________________________________

**Use Context Clues**   You have been introduced to three vocabulary words from the article about good and evil. Those words are checked off in the Word List here. Under "Vocabulary Word" below, write the other seven words from the Word List. Use context clues to write a meaning for each word under "Your Prediction." Then check the meanings in the Word Wisdom Dictionary. Write the definition under "Dictionary Says."

| | Vocabulary Word | Your Prediction | Dictionary Says |
|---|---|---|---|
| 1 | | | |
| 2 | | | |
| 3 | | | |
| 4 | | | |
| 5 | | | |
| 6 | | | |
| 7 | | | |

**WORD LIST**

versus
ambiguous
transgression
banishment
vile
implacable
reprehensible
ethical
thwart
affirmative

**Choose the Correct Word** Write the vocabulary word in parentheses that best completes each sentence. Underline any part of the sentence that helped you make your choice.

**1** Brett's _________________ outlook on life is just one aspect of his upbeat personality. (affirmative, reprehensible)

**2** During her years of _________________, the woman missed her home and family. (banishment, transgression)

**3** For Tim, the issue was an _________________ one: He wanted to do the right thing. (implacable, ethical)

**4** My dad's advice was so _________________ that I didn't know what to do. (implacable, ambiguous)

**5** When the situation involves an older sibling _________________ a younger one, does the older one always win? (versus, thwart)

**Select the Answers**   Read each question. Underline the best answer.

**6** Which of these would most people say is **reprehensible**?
a. giving money to charity
b. taking what isn't yours

**7** Which of these people would probably be **implacable**?
a. a child playing with a friend
b. a worker who must meet a challenging deadline

**8** Which of these is a **transgression**?
a. driving faster than the speed limit allows
b. keeping one's house in good order

**9** Which of these would most people call **vile**?
a. garbage rotting in the sun
b. a shabby, run-down piece of property

**10** Which of these is a way to **thwart** someone?
a. make the person feel calm
b. refuse to do something the person wants

**Use the Clues** Write a word from the Word List on page 120 that is close in meaning to each common saying, cliché, or idiom.

**1** Tom gave *a thumbs up* to our new idea.

_______________________________________________

**2** Although she understood the math concept, her explanation to me was

*as clear as mud.* ______________________________

**3** I completely trust my brother because he is *right as rain* and *as good as gold.*

_______________________________________________

**4** There was little hope of changing the criminal, as he seemed *rotten to the core.*

_______________________________________________

**5** The teachers were *dead set* in their decision to give the exams early.

_______________________________________________

**Answer the Questions** Answer each question.

**6** How might you **thwart** someone who was trying to upset you? ______________

_______________________________________________

**7** What might you say to someone who behaves in a **reprehensible** way? __________

_______________________________________________

**8** When might someone commit a **transgression**? ______________________

_______________________________________________

**9** How might you respond to the **banishment** of a family member? ____________

_______________________________________________

**10** Where would you most likely see the word *versus* in the newspaper? __________

_______________________________________________

**Write It!** Summarize a folktale, fairy tale, or legend that you especially like. Use as many words from the Part 1 Word List as you can.

# PART 2

# Latin Roots

*for Word Wisdom*

## A Pat on the Back:
# Say Something Nice!

**Do you enjoy giving and receiving compliments? Many people feel uncomfortable in one or both of these situations. When they receive a compliment, they feel "unworthy," or they suspect that the other person is not being sincere. When they attempt to give a compliment, they feel awkward and unsure of what to say.**

Let's start with a basic question: Are compliments good or bad? Some people offer compliments all day long. Far from having an **aversion** to them, they enjoy sharing them. These people begin and end every interaction with another person with some form of **pleasantry** that often includes a compliment.

Other people consider compliments to be mere **platitudes** with little meaning. They do not enjoy being complimented, and they certainly aren't going to insult others by handing out insincere compliments to everyone. People like this have the **erroneous** opinion that all compliments are insincere. They think compliments are not an example of good communication. Instead, they are an **aberration** from clear, honest communication. This group of people views compliments as **subversive** and manipulative, an attempt to flatter someone before asking for a favor.

A third group of people enjoys receiving compliments and thinks they deserve them. Nevertheless, this group is so **complacent** that they never think to compliment others.

Even if you are **erratic** about giving and receiving compliments, you can become more comfortable with them if you follow these tips:

1. Avoid offering phony compliments. If you don't mean it, don't say it. If you don't like your friend's new haircut, for example, don't say it looks great. In the same way, don't use a compliment to disguise or soften bad news. For example: "I really like the shirt you gave me, but I think I'll return it." That kind of compliment also sounds phony.

2. Be specific in your compliments. A comment such as "Your story was great!" seems hollow. You can make the compliment sound sincere by naming what you specifically liked. For example, you might say, "I especially liked the end of your story because Carly still wasn't sure what was real and what wasn't."

3. When someone compliments you, just say, "Thank you" or "I'm glad you liked it." You don't have to mumble, "Oh, it was nothing." If you suspect a compliment was insincere or was meant to flatter, say, "Thank you" anyway and forget about it.

Honest compliments show respect and thoughtfulness. If someone is dealing with some sort of **adversity,** offer a sincere compliment about that person's ability to deal with the challenge. A habit of giving compliments can help you emphasize what's right in the world, instead of focusing on others' **errant** behavior. Experiment with giving and receiving compliments until it becomes part of your daily interactions with the world. You and others will benefit!

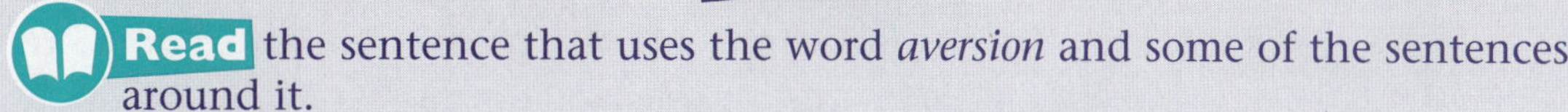

**Read** the sentence that uses the word *aversion* and some of the sentences around it.

**Look** for context clues to the word's meaning. What **Antonyms** can you find?

_______________________________________________

**Think** about the context clues and other information you already know.

_______________________________________________

**Predict** a meaning for the word *aversion*.

_______________________________________________

**Check** your Word Wisdom Dictionary to be sure of the meaning of the word *aversion*. Write the definition here.

_______________________________________________

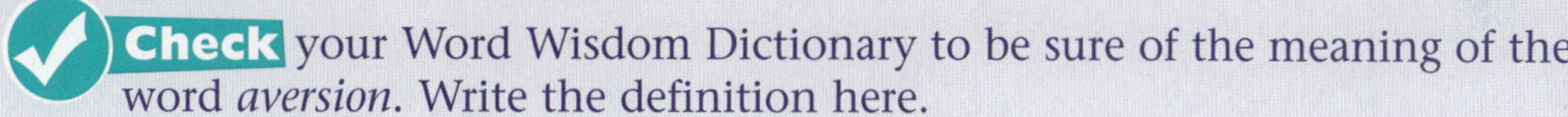

**Read** the sentence that uses the word *aberration* and some of the sentences around it.

**Look** for context clues to the word's meaning. What **Antonyms** can you find?

_______________________________________________

_______________________________________________

**Think** about the context clues and other information you may already know.

_______________________________________________

_______________________________________________

**Predict** a meaning for the word *aberration*.

_______________________________________________

**Check** your Word Wisdom Dictionary to be sure of the meaning of the word *aberration*. Write the definition here.

_______________________________________________

# Unlock the Meanings

Many English words have Latin roots. Knowing the meanings of roots can help you understand the meanings of many words. Many of the words you studied in Part 1 have Latin roots.

| Latin Root: **err** | Latin Root: **pla, plea** | Latin Root: **vers, vert** |
|---|---|---|
| meaning: to wander | meaning: to please | meaning: to turn |
| English word: *err* | English word: *implacable* | English word: *versus* |
| meaning: to make a mistake | meaning: determined | meaning: against |



**Categorize by Roots**  Find these roots in the Word List. Write each word under the correct root. Then circle the roots you find. Add other words you know that have the same roots.

## Good and Bad

| Latin Root: err | Latin Root: pla, plea | Latin Root: vers, vert |
|---|---|---|
| _______________ | _______________ | _______________ |
| _______________ | _______________ | _______________ |
| _______________ | _______________ | _______________ |
| _______________ | _______________ | _______________ |

| Prefix | Meaning |
| --- | --- |
| sub- | below |
| a- | not |

**Example**

**sub-** (below) + **vers** (turn) + **-ive** (adj.) = **subversive**

**Use Roots and Prefixes**   Circle any roots or prefixes that you find in the boldfaced words below. Use roots, prefixes, and context clues to write the meaning of each word. Check your definitions in the Word Wisdom Dictionary.

**1** The **subversive** pamphlet called for the overthrow of the dictator.

_______________________________________________

**2** Amy wanted to offer sincere thanks instead of some common **platitude**.

_______________________________________________

**3** The principal met with Jeff's parents to discuss Jeff's **errant** behavior.

_______________________________________________

**4** Was Teresa's lie an **aberration**, or was it typical of her?

_______________________________________________

**5** The worst **adversity** the family faced was being separated from one another.

_______________________________________________

**6** Saying "hello" or "good morning" can be an important **pleasantry**.

_______________________________________________

**7** The doctors had been misled by the **erroneous** research findings.

_______________________________________________

**8** After performing the difficult piano solo without an error, Krista became quite **complacent** about practicing.

_______________________________________________

**9** Phil had a great **aversion** to lima beans and refused to eat them.

_______________________________________________

**10** Sula's performance was **erratic**; no one could account for her perfection in some places and total failure in others.

_______________________________________________

WORD LIST

aversion

pleasantry

platitude

erroneous

aberration

subversive

complacent

erratic

adversity

errant

**Choose the Correct Word** Write the vocabulary word that best completes each sentence in the paragraph.

When Jonah's mom lost her job, the family experienced real

**1** _________________________ for the first time. They had always been

**2** _________________________ about their good fortune, but now all of that

suddenly changed. Even though it seemed like such an

**3** _________________________ for Jonah's mom not to go to work, after a

few weeks it seemed normal. Still, Jonah knew his mom would turn things

around sooner or later. Since she had such an **4** _________________________

to not working, she searched for a job with great determination. To say that

she was beaten or discouraged by the hardships was simply

**5** _________________________ .

**Write Sentences** Write a sentence that includes all of the words in each group. You may use the words in any order. You may also change the endings of words.

**6** subversive, plot, government _________________________

_________________________

**7** stealing, errant, behavior _________________________

_________________________

**8** exchange, pleasantries, neighbors _________________________

_________________________

**9** Brian, sorry, platitude _________________________

_________________________

**10** Sue, essay, erratic _________________________

_________________________

**Link to Your Life** Follow the instructions.

**1** Name one or more things to which you have an **aversion**. ______________
______________________________________________________________________

**2** Describe a time when you felt **complacent**. ______________________
______________________________________________________________________

**3** Name a **pleasantry** that you exchange regularly with your parents. ______
______________________________________________________________________

**4** Describe an **aberration** you have experienced or witnessed. ____________
______________________________________________________________________

**5** Explain some **adversity** you have experienced. ____________________
______________________________________________________________________

**Connect the Words** Write a word from the Word List to answer each question.

**6** Which word goes with saying a cliché and thinking it is meaningful?
______________________________________________________________________

**7** Which word goes with receiving three A's, one C, and one F?
______________________________________________________________________

**8** Which word goes with misprint or misstatement?
______________________________________________________________________

**9** Which word goes with secret plans? ______________________________

**10** Which word goes with an unusual, dishonest action?
______________________________________________________________________

**Speak It!** With a partner, role-play a conversation between two neighbors. Have them discuss local personalities as well as local news items. Use as many of the vocabulary words from this part as you can.

# PART 3

# Reference Skills



## Good or Bad?
# Cuba's Dictator

**Born in 1926, Fidel Castro has ruled Cuba since 1959, first as premier and then as president. In reality, he is a dictator. He does hold elections, but Cubans can vote only for him. Still, not everyone agrees about whether he is good or evil.**

Fidel Castro has a degree in law and worked as a lawyer from 1950 to 1952. In 1952, General Fulgencio Batista overthrew the Cuban government. Castro organized a small army and set up a **surreptitious** plan to take back control of Cuba. In the attack, however, many of his men were killed. Castro was sent to prison. After his release in 1955, Castro tried several more times to overthrow Batista. He finally succeeded in 1959.

At first, the United States supported Castro. This support ended when the Cuban government started to take over land belonging to American companies. Castro also began to buy oil from the Soviet Union, which didn't have a good relationship with the U.S. at the time. In 1961, Castro declared that he was a communist. The only legal political party in Cuba was the Communist Party.

Since then, the relationship between the United States and Cuba has been troubled. The U.S. attacked Cuba in 1961 at the Bay of Pigs. But, Castro captured the attackers and issued a **reproach** to the U.S. for this **sinister** plot.

Cuba is only about 90 miles south of Florida. Far from being an **exemplary** neighbor, Castro allowed the Soviet Union to assemble nuclear missiles in Cuba in 1962. In a tense stand-off called the Cuban Missile Crisis, the United States convinced Castro to stop, but relations continued to be hostile.

Until its collapse in 1990, the Soviet Union helped support Cuba. Since then, Cubans have suffered many hardships. This is partly due to an American ban on trade and travel with this nation.

But has Castro been a **benevolent** dictator or a tyrant? Some say he's a good leader. They point to Cuba's excellent education and health care systems. The nation's literacy rate is among the highest in Latin America. Cuba also telecasts college-level courses for adults. Few children are homeless, and all receive **sublime** health care.

However, instead of praising Castro, many people **lament** the lack of human rights in Cuba. Castro often sends his opponents to prison. He holds elections but runs unopposed. He censors the news and controls the press.

What would be a **felicitous** resolution of the friction between Cuba and the United States? Now that Castro is getting older, something must change. Looking somewhat **decrepit,** Castro still manages to give speeches that are hours long. They are filled with history as Castro sees it, not **levity**. At the same time, this dictator—benevolent or not—cannot rule forever.

**Practice the Context Clues Strategy** Here are two of the boldfaced words from the essay on page 128. Use the context clues strategy you learned in Part 1 on page 117 to figure out the meanings of these words.

## benevolent

**Read** the sentence that uses the word *benevolent* and some of the sentences around it.

**Look** for context clues to the word's meaning. What **Antonyms** can you find?

_______________________________________________

**Think** about the context clues and other information you already know.

_______________________________________________

**Predict** a meaning for the word *benevolent*.

_______________________________________________

**Check** your Word Wisdom Dictionary to be sure of the meaning of the word *benevolent*. Write the definition here.

_______________________________________________

## lament

**Read** the sentence that uses the word *lament* and some of the sentences around it.

**Look** for context clues to the word's meaning. What **Antonyms** can you find?

_______________________________________________

**Think** about the context clues and other information you already know.

_______________________________________________

**Predict** a meaning for the word *lament*.

_______________________________________________

**Check** your Word Wisdom Dictionary to be sure of the meaning of the word *lament*. Write the definition here.

_______________________________________________

## Dictionary Skills: Syllabication and Pronunciation

Dictionaries provide more than just meanings, forms of the words, and parts of speech. They also give the syllabication and pronunciation of entry words. The pronunciation is shown with special symbols that are explained in a chart like the one in your Word Wisdom Dictionary. Stressed syllables are shown with a special mark (´). Small dots (•) in the entry word are used to separate the word into syllables.

syllabication    stress mark

pleas•ant•ry / plĕz′ ən trē /

pronunciation

**Use the Dictionary** Draw a line between the syllables of each word below. Then circle the correct pronunciation. Check your answers in your Word Wisdom Dictionary.

| | | | |
|---|---|---|---|
| **1** | levity | lĕv′ ĭ tē | lĕv′ ă tē |
| **2** | sinister | sĭn′ īs tĕr | sĭn′ ĭ stər |
| **3** | lament | lə mĕnt′ | lă′ mĕnt |
| **4** | reproach | rĭ prōch′ | rĕ′ prōch |
| **5** | decrepit | də krĕp′ ăt | dĭ krĕp′ ĭt |
| **6** | felicitous | fĭ lĭs′ ĭ təs | fĕ lĭz′ ĭ tĭs |
| **7** | sublime | sə blime′ | sə blīm′ |
| **8** | benevolent | bə nĕv′ə lənt | bĕ nĕv′ lənt |
| **9** | surreptitious | sēr′ rĕp tĭsh′ ŭs | sûr′ əp tĭsh′ əs |
| **10** | exemplary | ĕg′ zĕm plə rē | ĭg zĕm′ plə rē |

**1.** Use context clues.

**2.** Look for a familiar root, prefix, or suffix.

**3.** If the context or a word part doesn't help, check the dictionary.

**WORD LIST**

surreptitious

reproach

sinister

exemplary

benevolent

sublime

lament

felicitous

decrepit

levity

**Define the Words** Follow the steps above to write the meaning of each boldfaced word. Then write 1, 2, or 3 to show which steps you used.

**1** When Katie was rude, her mother issued a swift **reproach**.

____________________________________________________

**2** Alone in his small boat on calm seas, the fisherman enjoyed the **sublime** power of the ocean.

____________________________________________________

**3** Vanessa was rewarded for her **exemplary** behavior.

____________________________________________________

**4** The **benevolent** teacher did not just preach kindness but also lived it.

____________________________________________________

**5** The **sinister** plot included actions that would destroy people's homes.

____________________________________________________

**6** Their **surreptitious** plan had to be carried out under the cover of night.

____________________________________________________

**7** The warm, sunny weather was **felicitous** for the picnic.

____________________________________________________

**8** The **decrepit** cabin was badly in need of paint and repairs.

____________________________________________________

**9** Everyone enjoys Dylan's **levity** and the lighthearted way he makes people laugh.

____________________________________________________

**10** Erica **lamented** the loss of the ring handed down by her grandmother.

____________________________________________________

**Find the Antonyms** Write the vocabulary word that is an antonym or near antonym for each underlined word.

**WORD LIST**
- surreptitious
- reproach
- sinister
- exemplary
- benevolent
- sublime
- lament
- felicitous
- decrepit
- levity

**1** After her performance, her father's <u>praise</u> was exactly what she expected.

_______________________________________________

**2** This did not seem to be the right occasion for so much <u>seriousness</u>.

_______________________________________________

**3** Everyone had heard stories about that <u>cruel</u> ruler.

_______________________________________________

**4** Mark's speech was especially <u>unsuitable</u> for the occasion.

_______________________________________________

**5** Jackie had never expected to experience such <u>lowly</u> thoughts.

_______________________________________________

**Classify the Words** Add the correct word from the Word List to each group.

**6** sly, secret, _______________________________________________

**7** beyond reproach, blameless, _______________________________________________

**8** evil, vile, _______________________________________________

**9** shabby, worn, _______________________________________________

**10** grieve, show sorrow, _______________________________________________

**11** suitable, appropriate, _______________________________________________

**12** scolding, reprimand, _______________________________________________

**13** humor, playfulness, _______________________________________________

**14** impressive, magnificent, _______________________________________________

**15** kind, caring, _______________________________________________

# Apply What You've Learned

**Complete the Analogies**  Choose the correct word to complete each analogy. Write it in the blank.

**1** Kind is to **benevolent** as worried is to _________________________.
  a. friendly
  b. anxious
  c. rude
  d. inseparable

**2** Loss is to **lament** as win is to _________________________.
  a. gain
  b. inherit
  c. celebrate
  d. review

**3** Misdeed is to **reproach** as accomplishment is to _________________________.
  a. congratulations
  b. sympathy
  c. warning
  d. success

**4** Neglect is to **decrepit** as maintenance is to _________________________.
  a. cluttered
  b. well-maintained
  c. run-down
  d. antique

**5** Criminal is to **sinister** as hero is to _________________________.
  a. vile
  b. outstanding
  c. celebrated
  d. brave

**Complete the Sentences**  Complete each sentence.

**6** Ed's leaving the house in hiking boots proved **felicitous** because

_______________________________________________

**7** Some people experience a **sublime** feeling when they see

_______________________________________________

**8** During the emergency, Steve's behavior was **exemplary** because

_______________________________________________

**9** Everyone was in the mood for a little **levity** because

_______________________________________________

**10** The plan for finding the money was **surreptitious** because

_______________________________________________

**Write It!**  With a small group, create a story map for a mystery. Include brief descriptions of characters and settings as well as a list of main events. Use several Part 3 vocabulary words.

# Review

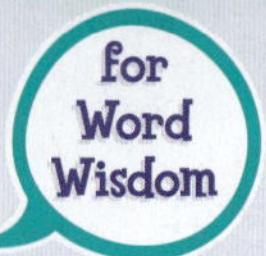


**Sort by Connotation** Decide if the words in the box below have positive or negative meanings, or connotations. Write the words from the box in the correct column.

| | | | |
|---|---|---|---|
| affirmative | banishment | ethical | adversity |
| benevolent | transgression | sublime | sinister |
| thwart | pleasantry | vile | aversion |
| subversive | reproach | exemplary | erratic |
| decrepit | | | |

| Positive | Negative |
|---|---|
| | |

## WORD LIST

- versus
- ambiguous
- transgression
- banishment
- vile
- implacable
- reprehensible
- ethical
- thwart
- affirmative
- aversion
- pleasantry
- platitude
- erroneous
- aberration
- subversive
- complacent
- erratic
- adversity
- errant
- surreptitious
- reproach
- sinister
- exemplary
- benevolent
- sublime
- lament
- felicitous
- decrepit
- levity

**Choose the Correct Word** Write the word in parentheses
that correctly completes each sentence.

**1** Leon thought the strange actions were typical of the boy's behavior, but they

turned out to be a(n) ________________________. (aberration, reproach)

**2** Benito's ability to think clearly under such difficult conditions was

________________________. (exemplary, benevolent)

**3** Mrs. Dudley talked at length with Emma about her ________________________
actions on the night of the game. (decrepit, errant)

**4** The situation did not call for ________________________; instead, it called for
a sincere and thoughtful dialogue. (transgressions, platitudes)

**5** We felt there was a ________________________ atmosphere in the dark alley.
(sinister, sublime)

**Use the Words Correctly in Writing** Rewrite each sentence in your own
words. Use the word in parentheses in your sentence. You may need to add an
ending to the word.

**6** Elena was lucky she didn't land in jail for her actions. (reprehensible)

________________________________________________________________

**7** The Redbirds had expected to win all along. (complacent)

________________________________________________________________

**8** The group was planning to disrupt daily operations at the ministry of justice.
(subversive)

________________________________________________________________

**9** How terrible Fumiyo felt about the loss of her pet dog Sandy! (lament)

________________________________________________________________

**10** The principal delivered a strong criticism of Jess's actions. (reproach)

________________________________________________________________

# Taking Vocabulary Tests

Never begin a test without reading the directions and the sample item carefully. One trap you can easily fall into is choosing a synonym instead of an antonym or vice versa. When a test asks for antonyms, the test writers will sometimes include a synonym as one of the choices. Don't let that confuse you! Stay alert and follow the directions.

**Sample:**

Fill in the letter of the item that most nearly means the OPPOSITE of the boldfaced word.

**benevolent**

Ⓐ kindly
Ⓑ unkind
Ⓒ generous
Ⓓ pure

**Practice Test**  Fill in the letter of the item that most nearly means the OPPOSITE of the boldfaced word.

**1 lament**
Ⓐ regret
Ⓑ despair
Ⓒ repair
Ⓓ rejoice

**2 levity**
Ⓐ joy
Ⓑ lightheartedness
Ⓒ lethargy
Ⓓ seriousness

**3 adversity**
Ⓐ disaster
Ⓑ hardship
Ⓒ good fortune
Ⓓ helpfulness

**4 surreptitious**
Ⓐ sly
Ⓑ noticeable
Ⓒ hopeful
Ⓓ disturbed

**5 affirmative**
Ⓐ constructive
Ⓑ full of despair
Ⓒ exhausted
Ⓓ negative

**6 erroneous**
Ⓐ correct
Ⓑ phony
Ⓒ slightly delayed
Ⓓ mistaken

**7 ethical**
Ⓐ moral
Ⓑ spiritual
Ⓒ immoral
Ⓓ displeased

**8 felicitous**
Ⓐ difficult
Ⓑ easy
Ⓒ suitable
Ⓓ unsuitable

**9 erratic**
Ⓐ unstable
Ⓑ uneven
Ⓒ mistaken
Ⓓ consistent

**10 aversion**
Ⓐ strong dislike
Ⓑ tendency
Ⓒ love
Ⓓ hatred

**Reconstruct the Meanings**  In each of the following sentences, one or more words are represented by only their first letter. If the letter is boldfaced, it is the first letter of a vocabulary word in this unit. If it is not boldfaced, it might be any word at all! See how many sentences you can figure out.

**1** The answer to a complex problem is never b__ and w__; it is always **a**__.

_______________________________________________

**2** When Mark added 432 and 261, he came up with the **e**__ answer of 683.

_______________________________________________

**3** The **b**__ man was so kind that he would give someone the s__ off his b__.

_______________________________________________

**4** Every day, Laura uttered this **p**__ to Mrs. Chu: "G__ m__, Mrs. Chu!"

_______________________________________________

**5** An **e**__ person knows r__ from w__.

_______________________________________________

**6** After years of **b**__ in a faraway country, the hero longed for h__ s__ h__.

_______________________________________________

**7** So many movies seem to have the same theme: the g__ guy **v**__ the b__ g__!

_______________________________________________

**8** Dr. Moretti had experienced many u__ and d__ in his **e**__ career.

_______________________________________________

**9** Although the task was huge, Ted was **i**__ as he shouted, "N__ or n__!"

_______________________________________________

**10** The **d**__ property seemed to suggest that its owners were d__ and o__.

_______________________________________________

**Speak It!**  With a partner, make a list of do's and don'ts for various social occasions and other situations in life. Use as many of the words from this unit as you can. Present your list to the class in a tone of voice that matches the advice.

# Context Clues



## Clocks:
# Telling Time Over Time

**The preoccupation with telling time reaches far back into history. Read this article to learn one part of the history of telling time—the history of clocks.**

How many times a day do you look at a clock or watch? In our modern **epoch,** humans are time-driven beings. We run our lives by schedules and by appointment books. We divide time into minutes, seconds, and even split seconds. People are in a rush, trying to hasten, speed up, and **expedite** every single task.

Although our human concern with the passing of the days and hours may be timeless, clocks are probably only 5,000 or 6,000 years old. One of the earliest clocks, the obelisk, was nothing more than a tall, stone needle. First used in ancient Egypt, this **primitive** clock cast shadows of different lengths at varying times of day. Later, the Egyptians developed the sun-dial, another device for telling time by the sun. Sundials, which were also used in other cultures, remained popular for several thousand years. By the tenth century A.D., fashionable people in Europe were carrying pocket sundials.

Sundials worked fairly well for telling approximate time on sunny days, but weren't useful on cloudy days or at night. To solve this problem, many cultures developed water clocks. In ancient Egypt and Greece, water clocks were stone containers with sloping sides and a hole in the bottom. The hole allowed water to drip out at a nearly constant rate. The sides of the container were marked with a series of lines; these **intervals** showed the passing of the hours.

In the **chronicle** of clock history, mechanical clocks were the next major development. They first appeared in the 1300s in Italy. Many took the form of huge clocks that tolled the hour, but they, too, were not very accurate. Mechanical clocks also took a smaller form. By the 1500s, the most fashionable people in Europe had replaced the **antiquated** sundial with the portable timepiece that we now call a watch. The first person to wear a watch on his wrist may have been the French mathematician Blaise Pascal. His "wristwatch" appears to have been an **impromptu** invention; it was simply his pocket watch tied to his wrist with a piece of string.

In contrast, most breakthroughs that gave rise to modern clocks were matters of **prolonged** research. The development of the pendulum clock, which took years, was a key step toward more reliable, precise clocks. **Subsequent** major developments have included the quartz clock and the atomic clock. Along the way have been countless lesser improvements ranging from the minute hand to the self-winding watch to the digital clock. New technologies rely on ever-more accurate clocks, so the search for better, more precise clocks is likely to go on for the next **millennium,** too.

# Context Clues Strategy

## Look for Objects or Ideas Related to the Word

**EXAMPLE:** We can count off time in hours and minutes, and we can also measure it in seconds and *nanoseconds*.

**CLUE:** This sentence names *hours*, *minutes*, and *seconds*, which are all units of time. By relating *nanoseconds* to these words, the sentence suggests that *nanoseconds* are a unit of time.

Here is another strategy for using context clues to figure out the meaning of the word *expedite* from the essay on page 138.

**Read** the sentence with the unknown word and some of the sentences around it.

*People are in a rush, trying to hasten, speed up, and* **expedite** *every single task.*

**Look** for context clues to the word's meaning. What **Objects or Ideas Related to the Word** can you find?

The words *in a rush, hasten,* and *speed up* are all related to the word *expedite*.

**Think** about the context clues and other helpful information you may already know.

I know that today, people do things faster than ever before. They try to get tasks done faster.

**Predict** a meaning for the word.

The word *expedite* must mean "to make faster or speed up."

**Check** your Word Wisdom Dictionary to be sure of the meaning.

The word *expedite* means "to get something done faster."

**Practice the Strategy** Two of the boldfaced words from the essay on page 138 are listed below. Use the context clues strategy on page 139 to figure out the meaning of each word.

## intervals

📖 **Read** the sentence that uses the word *intervals* and some of the sentences around it.

🔍 **Look** for context clues to the word's meaning. What **Objects or Ideas Related to the Word** can you find?

_______________________________________________

💡 **Think** about the context clues and other information you may know.

_______________________________________________

➡️ **Predict** a meaning for the word *interval*.

_______________________________________________

✔️ **Check** your Word Wisdom Dictionary to be sure of the meaning of the word *interval*. Write the dictionary definition.

_______________________________________________

## millennium

📖 **Read** the sentence that uses the word *millennium* and some of the sentences around it.

🔍 **Look** for context clues to the word's meaning. What **Objects or Ideas Related to the Word** can you find?

_______________________________________________

💡 **Think** about the context clues. What other information do you know?

_______________________________________________

➡️ **Predict** a meaning for the word *millennium*.

_______________________________________________

✔️ **Check** a dictionary to be sure of the meaning of the word *millennium*. Write the dictionary definition.

_______________________________________________

**WORD LIST**

epoch
✔ expedite
primitive
✔ interval
chronicle
antiquated
impromptu
prolong
subsequent
✔ millennium


**Use Context Clues** You have been introduced to three vocabulary words from the essay about clocks. Those words are checked off in the Word List. Under "Vocabulary Word" below, write the remaining seven words from the Word List. Use context clues to predict a meaning for each word under "Your Prediction." Then check the meanings in the Word Wisdom Dictionary. Write the definition under "Dictionary Says."

| | Vocabulary Word | Your Prediction | Dictionary Says |
| --- | --- | --- | --- |
| 1 | | | |
| 2 | | | |
| 3 | | | |
| 4 | | | |
| 5 | | | |
| 6 | | | |
| 7 | | | |

**WORD LIST**

- epoch
- expedite
- primitive
- interval
- chronicle
- antiquated
- impromptu
- prolong
- subsequent
- millennium

**Choose the Correct Words**   Write the vocabulary word that completes each sentence in the paragraph. You will need to add an ending to some words. Check a dictionary if you are not sure of the spelling.

One way to create a **1** ________________ of a period in history is by means of a well-developed time line. Time lines can be used to show periods of history ranging from days and months to centuries and **2** ________________. No matter how long the **3** ________________ they show, however, all time lines make use of **4** ________________. The first of these is marked at the farthest left point or at the top of the time line. **5** ________________ dates are shown in order by moving to the right or down the time line.

**Find the Antonyms**   Write the word from the Word List that is the opposite or most nearly the opposite of the underlined word in each sentence.

**6** The well-planned performance did not please the fussy audience.

________________

**7** The first cars quickly became modernized as new, improved models took their place. ________________

**8** Some people criticized the performance for being too brief.

________________

**9** Is the government planning to delay the release of the information?

________________

**10** Hector was stunned by how sophisticated the people's homes appeared to be. ________________

# Apply What You've Learned

**Order the Terms**  Write a word from the Word List that completes the sequence of ideas. You will need to add an ending to one word.

**1** previous, present, _______________________

**2** brief, moderately long, _______________________

**3** decade, century, _______________________

**4** futuristic, current, _______________________

**Classify the Words**  Write the vocabulary word that belongs in each group.

**5** simple, crude, _______________________

**6** narration, retelling, _______________________

**7** unplanned, spontaneous, _______________________

**8** era, age, _______________________

**9** space, time span, _______________________

**10** accelerate, hasten, _______________________

**Match the Synonyms**  Match each vocabulary word in the left column with its synonym in the right column. Write the letter of the correct synonym on the line.

| Vocabulary Word | Synonym |
| --- | --- |
| _______ **11** epoch | a. account |
| _______ **12** primitive | b. following |
| _______ **13** antiquated | c. period |
| _______ **14** chronicle | d. outdated |
| _______ **15** subsequent | e. unsophisticated |

**Write It!**  Imagine life in the next millennium. Give that time period a name. Describe some of the things people in that era might do or not do. Try to use most of the words from the Part 1 Word List.

# Latin and Greek Roots 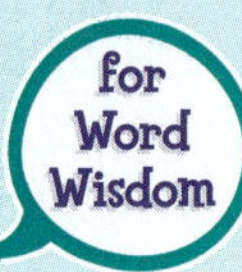



# Is Time Travel Possible?

**Can anyone actually move forward or backward in time? Many books, computer games, and movies use time travel to transport characters to a different time period.**

Some people insist that time travel belongs only in books, computer games, and movies. It is purely fictional. They point out that no one has discovered any **anachronisms** that prove people from other time periods have visited the current one. If time travel were possible, wouldn't someone from the past or future accidentally leave an object of some kind in the wrong time period?

Other people insist that we do have anachronisms. For example, perhaps the pyramids were built with technology from the future. Maybe the legendary city of Atlantis was a **prototype** for cities of the future. Maybe it had to be buried deep under the ocean to hide an anachronism. Maybe Leonardo da Vinci was actually a visitor from the future. After all, he drew helicopters centuries before anyone could have built one.

A few people think we have found few or no anachronisms because "time police" carefully control time travel. These police correct mistakes, picking up any items accidentally left behind. Their goal is to prevent any investigations that might **ensue** if the items were identified as being from another time period.

Or perhaps only people who are willing to follow a strict **protocol** are allowed to travel backward or forward in time. These people would be trained not to leave behind any clues to their presence. Their appearance out of **chronological** order would be cleverly disguised. The rest of us would not even notice anything out of the ordinary.

Naturally, we could not expect an organism from **primordial** time to travel to the future. The slime and ooze that existed back then had a **chronic** problem just existing from day to day. Wanting to travel ahead in time requires being aware that there is a future. The single-celled organisms that lived then had no concept of time or the **sequence** of events.

On the other hand, maybe people did travel from the future back to **primeval** times. With no written history from that time, events that took place back then were not recorded.

Of course, time travel would not be easy. Physics experts point out that Earth is a moving platform. It rotates on its axis as it revolves around the sun. If you moved ahead in time, you might materialize in thin air or in outer space. Thus, time travel would have to be carefully **synchronized** with Earth's movements.

Considering all the problems, time travel is not likely to be the "way to go" soon. Still, it's fun to imagine!

**Practice the Context Clues Strategy**  Here are two of the boldfaced words from the essay on page 144. Use the context clues strategy you learned in Part 1 on page 139 to figure out the meanings of these words.

## anachronisms

**Read** the sentence that uses the word *anachronisms* and some of the sentences around it.

**Look** for context clues to the word's meaning. What **Objects or Ideas Related to the Word** can you find?

___________________________________________

**Think** about the context clues and other information you already know.

___________________________________________

**Predict** a meaning for the word *anachronism*.

___________________________________________

**Check** your Word Wisdom Dictionary to be sure of the meaning of the word *anachronism*. Write the definition here.

___________________________________________

## synchronized

**Read** the sentence that uses the word *synchronized* and some of the sentences around it.

**Look** for context clues to the word's meaning. What **Objects or Ideas Related to the Word** can you find?

___________________________________________

**Think** about the context clues and other information you already know.

___________________________________________

**Predict** a meaning for the word *synchronize*.

___________________________________________

**Check** your Word Wisdom Dictionary to be sure of the meaning of the word *synchronize*. Write the definition here.

___________________________________________

Many English words have Latin or Greek roots. Knowing the meanings of roots can help you understand the meanings of many words. Some of the words you studied in Part 1 have Latin or Greek roots. Each root below is related to time.

| | | |
|---|---|---|
| **Greek Root: chron**<br>meaning: time<br>English word: *chronicle*<br>meaning: a record of historical events presented in time order | **Latin Root: prim, prin, proto**<br>meaning: first<br>English word: *primitive*<br>meaning: at an early stage of civilization, simple | **Latin Root: sec, seq, sue**<br>meaning: to follow<br>English word: *subsequent*<br>meaning: following in time order, later |

**Categorize by Roots**  Find these roots in the Word List. Then write each word in the correct column. Add other words you know that come from these roots.

**WORD LIST**

- anachronism
- prototype
- ensue
- protocol
- chronological
- primordial
- chronic
- sequence
- primeval
- synchronize

| Greek Root: chron | Latin Root: prim, prin, proto | Latin Root: sec, seq, sue |
|---|---|---|
| | | |
| | | |
| | | |
| | | |
| | | |

**Time**

<table>
<tr><td>Prefix</td><td>Meaning</td></tr>
<tr><td>ana-</td><td>back or backward</td></tr>
<tr><td>en-</td><td>cause to be</td></tr>
</table>

**Example**

**ana-** (backward) + **chron** (time) + **-ism** (noun) = **anachronism**

**Use Roots and Prefixes**  Circle the root and any prefix you find in the boldfaced words below. Use context clues, roots, and prefixes to write the meaning of each word. Check your definitions in the Word Wisdom Dictionary.

**1** Today, lighting your house with oil lamps would be an **anachronism**.

_______________________________________________

**2** We know what happened before today, but we don't know what will **ensue**.

_______________________________________________

**3** Let's **synchronize** our watches so we can start at the same time.

_______________________________________________

**4** The teacher listed the **sequence** of events that led to the Civil War.

_______________________________________________

**5** Do you know the **protocol** for the presidential inauguration?

_______________________________________________

**6** After Nate created the **prototype**, all the other models could be built.

_______________________________________________

**7** I wrote the events in my story in **chronological** order.

_______________________________________________

**8** The fossil records help us understand **primeval** times.

_______________________________________________

**9** Phil had a **chronic** problem with losing his keys and was often locked out.

_______________________________________________

**10** Those **primordial** plants no longer exist because the climate has changed so much over millions of years.

_______________________________________________

## WORD LIST

- anachronism
- prototype
- ensue
- protocol
- chronological
- primordial
- chronic
- sequence
- primeval
- synchronize

**Choose the Correct Words**  Write the vocabulary word in parentheses that correctly completes each sentence.

**1** The driver didn't know what trouble would ______________________ when she made the U-turn. (synchronize, ensue)

**2** The film recounted the historical events in ______________________ order. (chronological, primordial)

**3** There was much diplomatic ______________________ during the prime minister's visit. (sequence, protocol)

**4** Did those trees exist in ______________________ times? (chronic, primeval)

**5** Designers improved on the ______________________ to create better models. (prototype, anachronism)

**6** Please arrange the data in a meaningful ______________________. (sequence, protocol)

**7** A horse-drawn buggy is a(n) ______________________ on a modern highway. (prototype, anachronism)

**8** The scientists tried to understand the ______________________ life form based on the evidence that remains. (primordial, chronological)

**9** Sanjeev changed his morning routine because he had a ______________________ problem with lateness. (sequential, chronic)

**10** When the dancers ______________________ their movements, a beautiful effect is created. (ensue, synchronize)

# Apply What You've Learned

**Find Examples** Each boldfaced word below is followed by two example sentences. Only one example is related to the word. Write E next to that example.

**1** **anachronism**
Eli wrote a paper called "From the Stone Age to the Computer Age." _______

Eli wrote about the use of computers during the Stone Age. _____

**2** **primeval**
That evidence has been analyzed and dated in the laboratory. _______

That evidence dates from before the days of the dinosaurs. _____

**3** **ensue**
The investigation was launched following the mysterious disappearance. _____

The investigation focused on three locations in the city. _______

**4** **protocol**
There was a formal reception for the Secretary of State and her aides. _____

The Secretary of State has replaced several of her aides. _______

**5** **chronological**
The main meal will be at 6:00 P.M.; earlier meals will be served at 9:00 A.M. and 1:00 P.M. _______

Meals will be served at 9:00 A.M., 1:00 P.M., and 6:00 P.M. _____

**Use the Clues** Write the vocabulary word that best matches each clue.

**6** 1, 2, 3 or A, B, C _________________________________________________

**7** together in time _________________________________________________

**8** again, and again, and again _________________________________________

**9** from the land where time began ______________________________________

**10** the first light bulb _______________________________________________

**Speak It!** Work with a partner to role-play an interview with someone who lived long ago. The person taking the part of the reporter should prepare at least four questions that include words from the Part 2 Word List.

# Reference Skills

for Word Wisdom

## The Quest for Old Age:
# Healthy Living, Longer Life

**How long do you hope or expect to live? The number of years you live depends on many factors, some of which are under your control and some of which are not.**

The average human life span is not **immutable;** it has changed considerably over the past century. In 1900, the average person lived to be only forty-seven years old, but in 2003 the average person lived to be seventy-seven. Many more people who are alive today will live to be one hundred than in previous generations.

When we examine **longevity,** one factor takes **precedence** over all the others. That factor is gender. Women live longer than men. A second important factor is family history. The longer your ancestors lived and the fewer health problems they had, the longer and healthier your life is likely to be.

Although your gender and family history are out of your control, you are in charge of many other factors that can extend or **curtail** your life. One of the most important factors is your blood pressure. You can prolong your life by knowing your blood pressure, exercising, and eating right to keep it at a normal level.

Being overweight is a **perpetual** problem for many people and can be a **prelude** to diabetes, heart disease, and other serious medical problems. All of these problems can shorten your life, of course. The two best approaches to controlling your weight must be **simultaneous:** you must exercise and eat a healthy diet at the same time. Doing one but not the other is not nearly as effective as doing both together.

Despite all that is known about the dangers of tobacco smoke, death from smoking is a **perennial** fact. More than 400,000 people die every year because they, or someone close to them, smokes. People who have started smoking should quit and give their bodies a **reprieve** from poor health and lung disease, including lung cancer.

Some of these health problems might seem far in the future to you, but your life can end much too early if you do not heed this advice:

- Drive carefully, and remember that car accidents are the leading cause of death for Americans between the ages of six and twenty-seven. Wear a seatbelt whenever you are in a car.
- Do not use drugs. Drugs can lead to death directly because of their effects and side effects, and they can cause death indirectly because of their effect on the user's thinking and judgment.

One day, **posterity** may look back at us and wonder why so many people were careless with their health. Still, if you make wise choices in your life, you can improve your own longevity.

**Practice the Context Clues Strategy**   Here are two of the boldfaced words from the essay on page 150. Use the context clues strategy you learned in Part 1 on page 139 to figure out the meanings of these words.

### precedence

**Read** the sentence that uses the word *precedence* and some of the sentences around it.

**Look** for context clues to the word's meaning. What **Objects or Ideas Related to the Word** can you find?

_________________________________________________

**Think** about the context clues and other information you already know.

_________________________________________________

**Predict** a meaning for the word *precedence*.

_________________________________________________

**Check** your Word Wisdom Dictionary to be sure of the meaning of the word *precedence*. Write the definition here.

_________________________________________________

### simultaneous

**Read** the sentence that uses the word *simultaneous* and some of the sentences around it.

**Look** for context clues to the word's meaning. What **Objects or Ideas Related to the Word** can you find?

_________________________________________________

**Think** about the context clues and other information you already know.

_________________________________________________

**Predict** a meaning for the word *simultaneous*.

_________________________________________________

**Check** your Word Wisdom Dictionary to be sure of the meaning of the word *simultaneous*. Write the definition here.

_________________________________________________

**Dictionary Skills: Multiple Meanings** Many words have more than one definition. The dictionary numbers these definitions. Read these definitions of two words with more than one meaning.

1. **prel•ude**[1] /prĕl′ yood′ or prā′ lood′ or prē′ lood′/ *n.* an introductory event that comes before something more important.
2. **prel•ude**[2] /prĕl′ yood′ or prā′ lood′ or prē′ lood′/ *n.* a piece of music or an introduction to a piece of music.

1. **re•prieve**[1] /rə prēv′/ *n.* postponement or cancellation of punishment.
2. **re•prieve**[2] /rə prēv′/ *n.* temporary relief.

**Choose the Correct Meaning** Write **1** or **2** to show which meaning applies to the underlined word.

______ **1** The audience applauded enthusiastically at the conclusion of the <u>prelude</u>.

______ **2** The governor granted the prisoner a <u>reprieve</u> and set him free.

______ **3** My sneezes were a <u>prelude</u> to a bad cold.

______ **4** After a brief <u>reprieve</u> for lunch, the workers returned to the factory.

______ **5** I was afraid that his smile was just a <u>prelude</u> to his asking for a favor.

**Find Multiple Meanings** The two boldfaced words below also have more than one meaning. Look up both words in the Word Wisdom Dictionary. Write the two different meanings of each word. Write a sentence using one of the words.

**6** perennial ______________________________________________

**7** perennial ______________________________________________

**8** perpetual ______________________________________________

**9** perpetual ______________________________________________

**10** ______________________________________________

______________________________________________

**Find the Meaning**

1. Use context clues.
2. Look for a familiar root, prefix, or suffix.
3. If the context or a word part doesn't help, check the dictionary.



**Define the Words** Follow the steps above to write the meaning of each boldfaced word. Then write 1, 2, or 3 to show which steps you used.

**1** Lisa needed to **curtail** her spending in order to save money.

______________________________________________

**2** If two jobs need to be done, which one takes **precedence**?

______________________________________________

**3** The pattern of the seasons is **immutable**.

______________________________________________

**4** Because directing traffic is stressful, the officers get a **reprieve** every hour.

______________________________________________

**5** Dan's **perpetual** nagging drove his brothers crazy.

______________________________________________

**6** It was no surprise when Grandma turned 100; **longevity** runs in my family.

______________________________________________

**7** Lightning and rain are often **simultaneous**.

______________________________________________

**8** That old wedding dress has been restored and preserved for **posterity**.

______________________________________________

**9** A darkening sky is often a **prelude** to a storm.

______________________________________________

**10** The safety of bicyclists and pedestrians is a **perennial** issue in every big city.

______________________________________________

**Use the Words Correctly in Writing**  Rewrite each sentence in your own words. Use the word in parentheses in your sentence. You will have to add an ending to one word.

**1** Those family treasures are being saved for future generations. (posterity)

______________________________________________

______________________________________________

**2** The appetizers were the beginning of an unforgettable dinner. (prelude)

______________________________________________

______________________________________________

**3** Because of the budget cuts, we lost some after-school activities. (curtail)

______________________________________________

______________________________________________

**4** Hurricanes and earthquakes are reminders of nature's power. (perpetual)

______________________________________________

______________________________________________

**5** Preparing for the exam is more important than doing an extra credit project. (precedence)

______________________________________________

______________________________________________

**Use the Clues**  Write a vocabulary word that is related to each clue.

______________  **6** Our team wins the championship every year.

______________  **7** Happy 100th Birthday!

______________  **8** Give me a break!

______________  **9** Here we go again. It never changes.

______________  **10** All together now.



---

**WORD LIST**

immutable

longevity

precedence

curtail

perpetual

prelude

simultaneous

perennial

reprieve

posterity

**Relate the Meanings**  Use what you have learned to answer the questions or follow the directions. Answer in complete sentences.

**1** Name something that is a **perpetual** source of joy for parents.

_______________________________________________

**2** What would have to happen in order for you to get a **reprieve** from homework?

_______________________________________________

**3** What might a person say as a **prelude** to reporting bad news?

_______________________________________________

**4** Name something that is a **perennial** event in your town or city.

_______________________________________________

**5** In planning for a career, what issues would you give **precedence** to?

_______________________________________________

**6** What daily activities would be **curtailed** during a power failure?

_______________________________________________

**7** What is something people do for the sake of **posterity**?

_______________________________________________

**8** Why do many people think of **longevity** as a good thing?

_______________________________________________

**9** What is something you would call **immutable**? Why?

_______________________________________________

**10** What are two things that people often do **simultaneously**?

_______________________________________________

**Write It!** With a partner, write a description of what you might include in a time capsule. Imagine that the capsule will be opened in 100 years. Use as many of the words from the Part 3 Word List as you can.

# Review 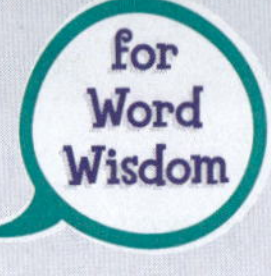



**Sort by Syllables and Find Roots** Write the words from the Word List in the correct column of the chart. Then circle the words that have the following prefixes you learned in Part 2: *chron, prim, prin, proto, sec, seq, sue.*

| 2 Syllables | 3 Syllables | 4 Syllables | 5 Syllables |
| --- | --- | --- | --- |
| | | | |

## WORD LIST

- epoch
- expedite
- primitive
- interval
- chronicle
- antiquated
- impromptu
- prolong
- subsequent
- millennium
- anachronism
- prototype
- ensue
- protocol
- chronological
- primordial
- chronic
- sequence
- primeval
- synchronize
- immutable
- longevity
- precedence
- curtail
- perpetual
- prelude
- simultaneous
- perennial
- reprieve
- posterity

**Classify the Words** Write the word from the Word List on page 156 that belongs in each group of words. Sometimes there may be more than one correct answer.

**1** out-of-date, old-fashioned, _______________________

**2** recurring often, lasting, _______________________

**3** original, model, _______________________

**4** future generations, descendants, _______________________

**5** earliest, ancient, _______________________

**Demonstrate Word Knowledge** Answer the questions or follow the directions.

**6** Tell why you would read a **chronicle**.

_______________________________________________

_______________________________________________

**7** Give an example of **protocol** at a wedding.

_______________________________________________

_______________________________________________

**8** What do you think has been the most interesting **epoch** in American history?

_______________________________________________

_______________________________________________

**9** The prefix *inter-* often means "between." Explain how this prefix helps you understand the meaning of **interval**.

_______________________________________________

_______________________________________________

**10** How is a **reprieve** from your duties different from a release from your duties?

_______________________________________________

_______________________________________________

# Taking Vocabulary Tests



Taking a test involves more than knowing the answers. It also involves managing your time. Before you begin, be sure you know how much time you have. Save a small amount of that time for review, and then determine how much time you have per item. If you find yourself taking too much time on any one item, move on. If you find yourself racing through the test, you may want to slow down.

## Sample:

Fill in the letter of the answer that BEST completes the analogy.

ending : conclusion : : prelude :

Ⓐ restatement
Ⓑ sequel
Ⓒ narrative
Ⓓ introduction

**Practice Test**  Fill in the letter of the answer that BEST completes the analogy.

**1** simple : complex : : primitive :
Ⓐ sophisticated
Ⓑ crude
Ⓒ poor
Ⓓ original

**2** reasonable : logical : : impromptu :
Ⓐ unreasonable
Ⓑ illogical
Ⓒ unplanned
Ⓓ undesirable

**3** century : hundred : : millennium :
Ⓐ thousandth
Ⓑ hundredth
Ⓒ thousand
Ⓓ ten thousand

**4** rules : sport : : protocol :
Ⓐ birthday
Ⓑ game
Ⓒ ceremony
Ⓓ party

**5** harmonize : music : : synchronize :
Ⓐ era
Ⓑ history
Ⓒ time line
Ⓓ time

**6** retreat : advance : : curtail :
Ⓐ extend
Ⓑ deliberate
Ⓒ stop short
Ⓓ repeat

**7** brief : momentary : : perpetual :
Ⓐ temporary
Ⓑ continuous
Ⓒ long
Ⓓ short

**8** immature: childish : : immutable :
Ⓐ variable
Ⓑ distant
Ⓒ unchangeable
Ⓓ youthful

**9** previous : before : : subsequent :
Ⓐ after
Ⓑ forward
Ⓒ backward
Ⓓ past

**10** reply : response : : reprieve :
Ⓐ reserve
Ⓑ respect
Ⓒ relief
Ⓓ report

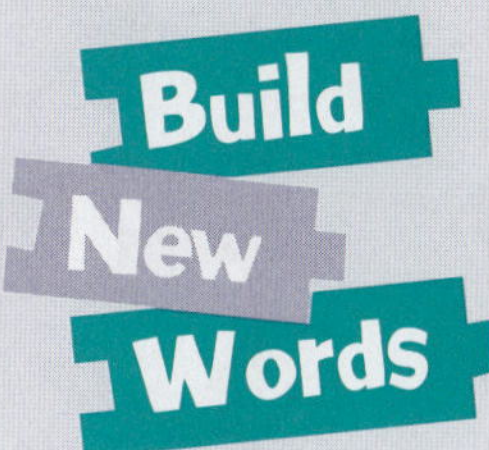

**Build New Words**

**Add a Prefix** The prefix *in-* usually means "not." When added to a word, it reverses the meaning of the word. You may not always recognize the *in-* prefix because its spelling changes when added to certain words or roots. For example, when added to the word *mutable* it is spelled *im-*.

**in-** (not) + **mutable** (changeable) = **immutable**

The *in-* prefix also changes to *im-* when added to words or roots beginning with *p* and *b*. It changes to *ir-* when added to words beginning with *r*, and to *il-* when added to words beginning with *l*.

Build new words by adding the *in-* prefix to the words below. Write the new word and its meaning.

| | | | | |
|---|---|---|---|---|
| **1** | in- | + patient = | | |
| **2** | in- | + movable = | | |
| **3** | in- | + balance = | | |
| **4** | in- | + responsible = | | |
| **5** | in- | + literate = | | |
| **6** | in- | + polite = | | |
| **7** | in- | + regular = | | |
| **8** | in- | + proper = | | |
| **9** | in- | + mature = | | |
| **10** | in- | + reverent = | | |

**Speak It!** Work in small groups to create a news broadcast "live" from the days of dinosaurs. Plan ways to introduce your newscast, report your news items, and conclude your story. Use as many words from this unit as you can. Then deliver your newscast to the class.

# Context Clues



## Laughter: A Funny Thing

We all know there's really no such thing as a funny bone, but few of us know why we laugh, or how we laugh, or even what's most likely to make us laugh. We do know, however, that it feels great to laugh, and we've all heard the saying that "laughter is the best medicine." Read this essay to learn more about laughter and the human mind.



Imagine the principal of your school as a high-school cheerleader. That's right: put him or her in the uniform, add a megaphone, and imagine jumps, splits, cheers, and all. Is that funny? Why?

Now think about why that image would make many people laugh. Psychologists, neurobiologists, and others who study laughter have determined three main causes for laughter. First, we laugh at things that are **incongruous,** like a dog ordering his dog bones online. The unexpected or unusual will often make us laugh.

Second, we also laugh at mistakes and whatever we personally regard as stupidity (and this is usually **subjective,** like most individual tastes). People who write sitcoms are well aware of these reasons for laughter and, as a result, tend to create a steady stream of **fatuous** errors and silly slip-ups. Finally, we laugh to get relief. When the mind feels stress or tension, it wants relief. Moviemakers constantly build this type of laughter into films, often by scripting some silliness into moments of high tension. In real life, when people laugh at inappropriate moments, this desire for relief is often the cause.

Many parts of the brain are involved in the production of laughter. The body gets in the act, too, and not just by means of the mouth. A good belly laugh involves your diaphragm, stomach, face, legs, and back muscles. It lowers blood pressure and raises your oxygen level. Also, like the effects of a good massage or great workout, laughter can be **therapeutic.** Psychiatrists credit it with releasing tension and helping to reduce stress. Physicians also **attribute** positive effects to laughter. Although the idea was once **refuted,** physicians now know that laughter even helps fight disease. In fact, they give **credence,** which is like approval, to a broad range of health benefits derived from laughter.

What else have scientists and researchers learned about laughter? It is widely believed that humans are the only species that **discerns** humor, the only species that laughs. On average, adult humans laugh about seventeen times a day. What we **deem,** or judge, to be funny is generally a matter of our age and level of maturity. We all know, for example, that toddlers enjoy a game of peek-a-boo more than the average adult does. We also know that laughter is contagious, but we do not know why. This may be because laughter acts like an impulse, or **stimulus,** for specialized receptors in the brain. Laughing in response to others' laughter may also have a social explanation. We share laughter as a way of belonging and filling a desire for companionship. In all, laughter is a funny thing and a good thing!

# Context Clues Strategy

## Look for What the Word Is Compared With

**EXAMPLE:** Many *marvels* of the mind, like other phenomena, are only partly understood.

**CLUE:** This sentence contains the key word *like*. This word alerts you to a comparison that is helpful in understanding the unfamiliar word. Marvels are *like other phenomena. Phenomena* means occurrences or events. Remember that comparisons give examples, associations, or related clues. In this sentence, marvels are mysterious, mental occurrences that cause wonder, surprise, or awe. They are like phenomena, which sometimes do this—and sometimes don't.

One way to learn new words is by studying the words that appear before and after them. Here is one strategy for using context clues to understand new words.

**Read** the sentence with the unknown word and some of the sentences around it.

*First, we laugh at things that are **incongruous**, like a dog ordering his dog bones online.*

**Look** for context clues to the word's meaning. What clues to **What the Word Is Compared With** do you find?

The sentence says that something that is *incongruous* is like a dog ordering his dog bones online.

**Think** about the context clues and other information you may already know.

I know that dogs definitely don't go online. I picture that in my mind, and it is funny because it is so unusual and unpredictable.

**Predict** a meaning for the word.

The word *incongruous* must mean "unexpected or unlikely."

**Check** your Word Wisdom Dictionary to be sure of the meaning.

The word *incongruous* means "not suitable; inappropriate or illogical."

**Practice the Strategy** Look at the two words from the essay on page 160. Use the context clues strategy on page 161 to figure out the meaning of each word.

## subjective

📖 **Read** the sentence that uses the word *subjective* and some of the sentences around it.

🔍 **Look** for context clues to the word's meaning. What clues to **What the Word Is Compared With** can you find?

_______________________________________________

💡 **Think** about the context clues. What other helpful information do you know?

_______________________________________________

➡️ **Predict** a meaning for the word *subjective*.

_______________________________________________

✔️ **Check** your Word Wisdom Dictionary to be sure of the meaning for the word *subjective*. Write the definition here.

_______________________________________________

## stimulus

📖 **Read** the sentence that uses the word *stimulus* and some of the sentences around it.

🔍 **Look** for context clues to the word's meaning. What clues to **What the Word Is Compared With** can you find?

_______________________________________________

💡 **Think** about the context clues. What other helpful information do you know?

_______________________________________________

➡️ **Predict** a meaning for the word *stimulus*.

_______________________________________________

✔️ **Check** your Word Wisdom Dictionary to be sure of the meaning for the word *stimulus*. Write the definition here.

_______________________________________________

**Use Context Clues**  You have been introduced to three vocabulary words from the laughter essay. Those words are checked off in the Word List here. Under "Vocabulary Word" below, write the other seven words from the Word List. Write a possible meaning for each word under "Your Prediction." Then check the meanings in the Word Wisdom Dictionary. Write the definitions under "Dictionary Says."

**WORD LIST**

- ✔ incongruous
- ✔ subjective
- fatuous
- therapeutic
- attribute
- refute
- credence
- discern
- deem
- ✔ stimulus

| | Vocabulary Word | Your Prediction | Dictionary Says |
|---|---|---|---|
| 1 | | | |
| 2 | | | |
| 3 | | | |
| 4 | | | |
| 5 | | | |
| 6 | | | |
| 7 | | | |

# Process the Meanings



**Choose the Correct Word**  Write the vocabulary word that completes each sentence in the paragraph.

### WORD LIST

incongruous

subjective

fatuous

therapeutic

attribute

refute

credence

discern

deem

stimulus

Most people like to go to the movies, but tastes in movies are varied and

**1** ________________________. Some people like only comedies, and some

prefer slapstick, although this is **2** ________________________ to others. Some

people **3** ________________________ comedies a waste of time and prefer

serious dramas instead. These viewers often **4** ________________________

more talent to a director of serious films than they do to a director of comedies.

For other moviegoers, it seems completely **5** ________________________ and

illogical to judge the worth of a film by whether it is serious or comic.

**Write the Sentences**  Write a sentence that uses all the words in each group. You may use the words in any order. You may also change the endings of words.

**6** therapeutic, benefits, exercise ________________________

________________________

**7** Mario, refute, argument ________________________

________________________

**8** discern, shape, darkness ________________________

________________________

**9** smell, stimulus, appetite ________________________

________________________

**10** facts, credence, theory ________________________

________________________

**11** success, Pam, attribute ________________________

________________________

**12** subjective, art, gallery ________________________

________________________

**Find Examples** Each word is followed by two sentences. Only one sentence suggests the meaning of the word correctly. Write **E** next to the example.

**1** incongruous:    Mother wore her winter coat with sandals. ______

Mother wore her winter coat with a scarf and hat. ______

**2** deem:    Mrs. Cole calls the work of three students "exceptional." ______

Three exceptional students work together on a project. ______

**3** subjective:    Irena relies on her own ideas to form a judgment. ______

Irena gathers a lot of data before she forms a judgment. ______

**4** discern:    Tim helps his brother become a team member. ______

Tim notices a change in how hard his brother works. ______

**5** credence:    Tiffany accepts Leo's version of the story. ______

Tiffany questions Leo's version of the story. ______

**6** therapeutic:    That stream is said to have curing properties. ______

That stream has grown steadily more polluted. ______

**7** fatuous:    The idea was so strange that we didn't respond to it. ______

The idea was so comical that we burst out laughing. ______

**8** attribute:    The meat was placed next to the sink. ______

The meat may have led to the outbreak of disease. ______

**9** stimulus:    Bright sunshine never fails to wake me up. ______

I wake up feeling refreshed every morning. ______

**10** refute:    People once believed that Earth was flat. ______

People believed for centuries that Earth was flat. ______

**Write It!** What is the most worthwhile part of your school day? In a fully developed paragraph, make a judgment, state it in a topic sentence, and support it. Use as many vocabulary words from Part 1 as you can.

# Latin Roots

for Word Wisdom

## Social Injustice:
## A Closed Mind

**Prejudice is a hostile attitude formed without just cause toward a group of people. Much prejudice is based on race, but prejudice can also be based on gender, age, appearance, income, education, and more.**

Why are some people prejudiced? Some people believe that prejudice is a natural part of our personalities. However, most experts now **reject** that theory. They are certain that prejudice is not part of anyone's personality. Instead, prejudice is learned. It often develops before the person has any real contact with the object of the prejudice. The person "prejudges" others without getting to know them.

Some prejudice develops when people feel uncertain about themselves. To make themselves feel better, they believe that their way of life and ways of thinking are superior. They reject anyone who is unlike them. They **confusedly** blame their problems and frustrations on people who are different from them in some way. Prejudiced people believe they are being fair and **objective**, but their opinions are based on faulty **conjectures**, such as assuming that an entire group is unfriendly because one member is shy. Prejudiced people are certain that most things in their life would be better if it weren't for this other group. Arguing against this position is usually **futile**. Prejudiced people are certain they have carefully thought the issue through. They stand by their **creed**, regardless of its shaky foundation.

Sometimes people become prejudiced by imitation. Perhaps someone they respect has a poor opinion of a certain group. They believe that this person's opinions are **credible** and admirable, so they become prejudiced, too. If presented with facts that **discredit** the prejudice, they ignore them. They are actually proud of their prejudice because they believe their opinion is correct and just.

It is easy to be **incredulous** when faced with another person's prejudice. How could this person think that way? Why can't he or she see things as they really are? Often, though, we fail to recognize or admit our own prejudices. We would be surprised and **confounded** if others pointed them out. We are certain that our opinions are based on facts and experience, not faulty assumptions.

If a prejudice is identified, how can it be overcome? If a prejudice is based on low self-esteem, gaining self-confidence can help the person let go of it. Often just getting to know the people who are the object of the prejudice helps considerably. When we get to know people as individuals, not as members of a group, we can better understand their strengths, needs, and motivations. We can eliminate the boundary that separates "us" from "them." We can open our minds and change our faulty reasoning.

Working together helps people get to know—and respect—each other. It's that simple.

## conjectures

**Read** the sentence that uses the word *conjectures* and some of the sentences around it.

**Look** for context clues to the word's meaning. What clues to **What the Word Is Compared With** can you find?

_______________________________________________

**Think** about the context clues. What other helpful information do you know?

_______________________________________________

_______________________________________________

**Predict** a meaning for the word *conjecture*.

_______________________________________________

**Check** your Word Wisdom Dictionary to be sure of the meaning of the word *conjecture*. Write the definition here.

_______________________________________________

## confounded

**Read** the sentence that uses the word *confounded* and some of the sentences around it.

**Look** for context clues to the word's meaning. What clues to **What the Word Is Compared With** can you find?

_______________________________________________

**Think** about the context clues. What other helpful information do you know?

_______________________________________________

**Predict** a meaning for the word *confound*.

_______________________________________________

**Check** your Word Wisdom Dictionary to be sure of the meaning of the word *confound*. Write the definition here.

_______________________________________________

Many English words have Latin roots. Knowing the meanings of roots can help you understand the meanings of many words. Many of the words you studied in Part 1 have Latin roots. Each root below is related to the mind.

> Latin Root: **cred**
> meaning: to trust, to believe
> English word: *credence*
> meaning: acceptance as true; belief

> Latin Root: **fus, fut**
> meaning: to disprove, to pour
> English word: *refute*
> meaning: to prove to be false or wrong

> Latin Root: **ject**
> meaning: to throw
> English word: *subjective*
> meaning: related to a point of view

**WORD LIST**

- reject
- confusedly
- objective
- conjecture
- futile
- creed
- credible
- discredit
- incredulous
- confound

**Categorize by Roots**  Find these roots in the Word List. Then write each word in the correct column. The spelling of the root may change in some words. Circle the roots in the words you write. Add other words you know that contain these roots.

## The Mind

| Latin Root: cred | Latin Root: fus, fut | Latin Root: ject |
| --- | --- | --- |
| _________ | _________ | _________ |
| _________ | _________ | _________ |
| _________ | _________ | _________ |
| _________ | _________ | _________ |
| _________ | _________ | _________ |

| Prefix | Meaning |
| --- | --- |
| ob- | toward, against |
| dis- | not |
| con- | with |

**Example**

**ob-** (against) + **ject** (throw) + **ive** = **objective**

**Use Roots and Prefixes**  Circle any roots or prefixes that you find in the boldfaced words below. Use your knowledge of roots, prefixes, and context clues to write the meaning of each word. Check your definitions in the Word Wisdom Dictionary.

**1** Jake tried to **discredit** Olivia's story even though he knew it was true.

_______________________________________________

**2** The new researcher looked **confusedly** at page after page of complicated data.

_______________________________________________

**3** You should gather a lot of facts if you hope to make an **objective** decision.

_______________________________________________

**4** Although the search for the missing cat seemed **futile** at first, we eventually found her.

_______________________________________________

**5** I suggested meeting at the park, but Phil **rejected** my idea.

_______________________________________________

**6** At the beginning of every club meeting, we recite our **creed**.

_______________________________________________

**7** When Sam heard how Yoko had won the lottery, he was **incredulous**.

_______________________________________________

**8** Some people did not believe Shania, but Mr. Freeman found her story **credible**.

_______________________________________________

**9** The lawyer could not base her case on **conjecture**; she needed evidence.

_______________________________________________

**10** The strange code **confounded** many historians, who could not unlock its meaning.

_______________________________________________

**WORD LIST**

reject

confusedly

objective

conjecture

futile

creed

credible

discredit

incredulous

confound

**Choose the Correct Word**  Write the vocabulary word that best completes each sentence. You will have to change the ending of a word.

**1** The opposing lawyer did her best to _________________________ the testimony of the star witness.

**2** Although the book was fiction, many events in it were realistic and _________________________.

**3** Swimming against a strong tide is _________________________; if you are in danger, tread water instead.

**4** Our _________________________ tells a great deal about who we are and what we value.

**5** The store _________________________ my application because I didn't have any experience.

**6** Did the criminals leave those false clues in an effort to _________________________ the police?

**7** We really admired Rick's explanation and reasoning, which were clear and _________________________.

**8** Sharmila's _________________________ seemed logical, but it was not the same as proof.

**9** The child stared _________________________ at the three doors and could not decide which to enter.

**10** Most of us were both speechless and _________________________ in response to the shocking news.

**Complete the Analogies**  Choose the word that completes each analogy. Write the correct word on the line.

**1** Give : receive :: **discredit** : _______________________.
a. think          b. deny          c. doubt          d. believe

**2** Theory : scientist :: **conjecture** : _______________________.
a. teacher        b. minister      c. mechanic       d. detective

**3** Distant : far away :: **futile** : _______________________.
a. hopeless       b. fearless      c. careless       d. thoughtful

**4** Hideous : beautiful :: **credible** : _______________________.
a. helpful        b. thankful      c. suspicious     d. thoughtful

**Relate the Meanings**  Use what you have learned about the boldfaced word to answer each question.

**5** What is one **creed** you try to live by? _______________________

_______________________________________________________________

**6** When might people **reject** an offer of help? _______________________

_______________________________________________________________

**7** How are the words *incongruous* and *confound* alike? _______________________

_______________________________________________________________

**8** Why would someone who saw a ten-foot rabbit feel **incredulous**? _______________

_______________________________________________________________

**9** Where might a person wander about **confusedly**? _______________________

_______________________________________________________________

**10** Why is it important for an umpire to be **objective**? _______________________

_______________________________________________________________

**Speak It!**  With a partner, brainstorm a list of helpful hints for finding and sorting through sources on the Internet. Use as many vocabulary words from Part 2 as you can. Deliver your list of tips to the class.

# Reference Skills

for Word Wisdom

## Personal Learning Style:
## How We Learn

**People learn in different ways. Knowing your personal learning style can help you learn more quickly and easily. There are three main types of learners: auditory, visual, and kinesthetic/tactile.**

Auditory learners depend on their sense of hearing and prefer to hear instructions rather than read them. These learners are so tuned to listening that they can become distracted by other noises. After meeting someone, auditory learners may soon forget the person's face, but they usually remember his or her name.

Visual learners focus on seeing. They prefer not to listen to long lectures—unless they include pictures or other illustrations. If something needs to be assembled, visual learners would rather study a diagram than listen to instructions. Movement and untidiness **contend** for their attention and are very distracting. Unlike auditory learners, visual learners tend to forget names but remember people's faces.

Your kinesthetic sense provides feedback from your bones and muscles as you move. The tactile sense is the sense of touch. Kinesthetic/tactile learners gain information by moving, touching, and doing. They use gestures to help them **elucidate** their feelings. Instead of listening to instructions or studying a diagram, they just begin a task and figure things out as they go. Some observers might **misconstrue** this approach as proof of impatience, but kinesthetic/tactile learners learn and perform better when they can manipulate things. When they meet someone, they might forget the name and the face. But they probably will recall the activity they did together when they met.

Some psychologists also categorize people by their preferred learning environments. Some learners do best when they work alone. They enjoy figuring things out independently. Some learners work best with others. For them, an invitation to be part of a study group is a **compelling** reason to prepare for a test.

Of course, you should not **surmise** that every person fits neatly into one of these categories. People usually learn better in one way than another, but they can learn in a variety of ways. The way we learn best depends on the subject matter, our mood at the time, our surroundings, and other factors.

No one needs to know about learning styles more than teachers. Long ago, colleges **indoctrinated** teachers with the idea that children should sit and listen. Students often struggled to learn facts by **rote,** like young robots. Now, just as college professors teach the subject matter that teachers will pass on to their students, they also **apprise** teachers of the various learning styles and encourage them to present information in a variety of ways. Teachers no longer **presume** that one way of teaching is best for all children. Their experience in the classroom **instills** a sense of respect for a variety of learning styles.

**Practice the Context Clues Strategy** Here are two of the boldfaced words from the essay on page 172. Use the context clues strategy you learned in Part 1 on page 161 to figure out the meanings of these words.

### rote

**Read** the sentence that uses the word *rote* and some of the sentences around it.

**Look** for context clues to the word's meaning. What clues to **What the Word Is Compared With** can you find?

_______________________________________________

**Think** about the context clues. What other helpful information do you know?

_______________________________________________

**Predict** a meaning for the word *rote*.

_______________________________________________

**Check** your Word Wisdom Dictionary to be sure of the meaning of the word *rote*. Write the definition here.

_______________________________________________

### apprise

**Read** the sentence that uses the word *apprise* and some of the sentences around it.

**Look** for context clues to the word's meaning. What clues to **What the Word Is Compared With** can you find?

_______________________________________________

_______________________________________________

**Think** about the context clues. What other helpful information do you know?

_______________________________________________

**Predict** a meaning for the word *apprise*.

_______________________________________________

**Check** your Word Wisdom Dictionary to be sure of the meaning of the word *apprise*. Write the definition here.

_______________________________________________

# Unlock the Meanings

**Dictionary Skills: Pronunciation Key** All dictionaries have pronunciation keys. You might find this key at the front of your dictionary or on each right-hand or left-hand page. It will tell you how to pronounce a new word by showing how sounds in that new word are pronounced in more familiar words. Here are some entries from a pronunciation key.

| | | |
|---|---|---|
| ă mat | ā may | âr dare |
| ə about | ĕ bet | ē me |
| o͝o book | zh vision | hw what |

**Find the Pronunciations** Circle the word that correctly completes each sentence. Use your Word Wisdom Dictionary to check your answer.

Example: The e in *contend* is pronounced like the e in (set)   easy

**1** The first e in *presume* is pronounced like the e in     pet    prevent

**2** The i in *misconstrue* is pronounced like the i in     hit    ice

**3** The i in *surmise* is pronounced like the i in     pine    spin

**4** The a in *apprise* is pronounced like the a in     able    about

**5** The o in *rote* is pronounced like the o in     go    gone

**Write the Words With the Same Pronunciation** Write a word that has the same pronunciation as that listed below. Use a dictionary to check your answer.

**6** The first i in *instill* is pronounced like the i in _______________.

**7** The u in *elucidate* is pronounced like the u in _______________.

**8** The a in *indoctrinate* is pronounced like the a in _______________.

**9** The o in *compelling* is pronounced like the o in _______________.

**10** The e in *contend* is pronounced like the e in _______________.

**Find the Meaning**

**1.** Use context clues.

**2.** Look for a familiar root, prefix, or suffix.

**3.** If the context or a word part doesn't help, check the dictionary.



**Define the Words** Use the steps above to determine the meaning of each boldfaced word. Write the meaning of the word. Then write 1, 2, or 3 to show which steps you used.

**1** Adam promised to **apprise** us of his decision so we could make plans.

_______________________________________________

**2** Those directions are so poorly written that it is easy to **misconstrue** them.

_______________________________________________

**3** Earning money is one of the most **compelling** reasons for going to work.

_______________________________________________

**4** Chung's job was to **indoctrinate** the new members of the group.

_______________________________________________

**5** Chelsea knew what she felt, but she could not **elucidate** her feelings to others.

_______________________________________________

**6** Because the work contained so many careless errors, Mr. Meterko **surmised** it had been done hastily.

_______________________________________________

**7** We were amazed when the four-year-old named all of the U.S. presidents by **rote**.

_______________________________________________

**8** Over the years, my mother **instilled** a sense of fairness and justice in me.

_______________________________________________

**9** The two semi-finalists will **contend** for the championship next Saturday.

_______________________________________________

**10** Jared often **presumes** that everyone is happy to hear from him.

_______________________________________________

**WORD LIST**

- contend
- elucidate
- misconstrue
- compelling
- surmise
- indoctrinate
- rote
- apprise
- presume
- instill

**Find the Synonyms**  Write the word from the Word List that is a synonym for the underlined word in each sentence.

**1** The teacher wanted to <u>implant</u> a love of learning in the minds of her young students. ______________________________

**2** We will take action as soon as the committee members <u>inform</u> us of their decision. ______________________________

**3** What could you <u>infer</u> about the character based on the first three words she spoke? ______________________________

**4** Luis is known for his kindness, so he must have had <u>powerful</u> reasons for being unfriendly to Max. ______________________________

**5** These essays help <u>explain</u> the theory behind each invention.

______________________________

**Choose the Correct Words**  Write the word in parentheses that completes each sentence. Underline any part of the sentence that helped you make your choice.

**6** My father said, "I ______________________________ you will clean this room within the hour!" (presume, apprise)

**7** Melinda's ______________________________ knowledge of division facts didn't impress me, because she was not a great problem solver. (rote, compelling)

**8** The leaders of our troop ______________________________ all new members by quickly teaching them the basic values and procedures under which we operate. (instill, indoctrinate)

**9** The best players will ______________________________ for the opportunity to represent our school at the national meeting. (contend, surmise)

**10** It was easy to ______________________________ the vague and careless instructions. (elucidate, misconstrue)

**Connect the Clues** Write a word from the Word List for each clue.

**1** It goes with "have to," "must," and "because I said so!"

_______________________________________________

**2** It goes with "clear as a bell." _______________________________

**3** It goes with "The two undefeated teams will meet in the championship game." _______________________________

**4** It goes with "by heart." _______________________________

**5** It goes with "this is just to inform you" and "for your information."

_______________________________________________

**Link to Your Life** Follow the instructions or answer the questions.

**6** What is one thing that a parent or other adult has **instilled** in you?

_______________________________________________

**7** What is something you regularly **presume** about your upcoming school day?

_______________________________________________

_______________________________________________

**8** What would you **surmise** if your teacher said, "I have good news for you!"

_______________________________________________

**9** Name something you could easily **misconstrue**. _______________________

_______________________________________________

**10** How might a group leader best **indoctrinate** a new member?

_______________________________________________

_______________________________________________

**Write It!** Describe situations in which people commonly act in the following ways: *apprise, elucidate, surmise, presume, instill,* and *indoctrinate.* For example, "The Secretary of State may apprise the President about a dangerous foreign situation." Address all six of these words from Part 3.

# Review 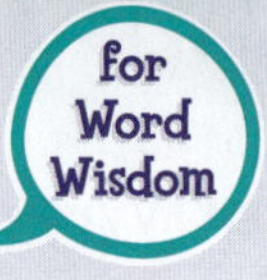



**Sort by Part of Speech** Decide whether each word in the Word List is a noun, verb, adjective, or adverb. Write each word in the correct column. Some words belong in more than one group.

## WORD LIST

- incongruous
- subjective
- fatuous
- therapeutic
- attribute
- refute
- credence
- discern
- deem
- stimulus
- reject
- confusedly
- objective
- conjecture
- futile
- creed
- credible
- discredit
- incredulous
- confound
- contend
- elucidate
- misconstrue
- compelling
- surmise
- indoctrinate
- rote
- apprise
- presume
- instill

| Noun | Verb | Adjective | Adverb |
|------|------|-----------|--------|
|      |      |           |        |

**Complete the Rhymes** Write the word from the Word List on page 178 that completes the meaning and the rhyme.

**1** A forceful kind of telling

could prove to be _________________!

**2** If you recite without referring to a single note,

then the chances are good that your knowledge is _________________.

**3** Each day I try to do at least one good deed;

doing good works is part of my _________________.

**4** Backwards, mixed up, and upside down:

these describe situations that are likely to _________________!

**5** A first-place title is something you have to defend,

so at the next championship you will have to _________________.

**Use the Words Correctly in Writing** Rewrite each sentence in your own words. Use the word in parentheses in your sentence.

**6** The first-grade teacher develops a love of reading in her students. (instill)

_______________________________________________

**7** We don't know where the suspect is, but we think he is in the area. (surmise)

_______________________________________________

**8** We are quite sure that we can trust our sources. (credible)

_______________________________________________

**9** Your analysis should reflect more data and varying points of view. (objective)

_______________________________________________

**10** The dog ran from one person to another, looking for its owner. (confusedly)

_______________________________________________

# Taking Vocabulary Tests

## TEST-TAKING STRATEGY

An important strategy when taking a multiple-choice test is to eliminate wrong answers. When you read the test question, you might not immediately know which answer is the right one, but you might know for sure that at least one choice is wrong. Eliminate that answer right away. If there are other answers you are reasonably sure are wrong, eliminate them, too. If the test items contain paragraphs, make sure to read the whole paragraph carefully.

### Sample:

Below is a short paragraph. Read the paragraph carefully. Then fill in the circle of the item that BEST defines the boldfaced word.

Mrs. Alpert considered my request, but not for long. She did not think the reasons I had given were convincing. Shaking her head "no," she wrote *rejected* at the top.

(A) denied
(B) postponed
(C) approved
(D) rewritten

---

**Practice Test** Below are five short paragraphs. Read each paragraph carefully. Then fill in the circle of the item that BEST defines the boldfaced word.

**1** Everything went wrong yesterday! I missed the school bus. I forgot my math homework. At home, I broke one of my mother's favorite dishes as I was setting the table. On top of it all, I had a fight with my best friend. I **deem** yesterday a day of disasters!

(A) regret   (B) interpret   (C) judge   (D) support

**2** We made several efforts to recover the lost document on the computer, but everything we did was **futile**. Late at night, Kara had no choice but to start over. How she regretted never having made a backup copy!

(A) useless   (C) too simple
(B) high-tech   (D) senseless

**3** First, Ian said he'd won the district championship. Then he said he'd gone on to win the county title. Next, seeming to have exaggerated, he said he had placed first in the state and was going to the Olympic trials! Of course, we were **incredulous**!

(A) happy   (C) doubtful
(B) admiring   (D) jealous

**4** Highway signs are difficult to write. They have to be extremely brief and easy to read. At the same time, they can't be too short or simple. If people **misconstrue** them, accidents are likely to result.

(A) translate   (C) ignore
(B) misunderstand   (D) stop to read

**5** During the hearing exam, the doctor realized that the patient could **discern** sounds far more easily with her right ear than with her left ear. This information helped the doctor both understand the patient's problems and communicate with her.

(A) create   (B) repeat   (C) listen to   (D) perceive

**Write What Words Would Say** If a word could talk, what would it say? Write a word from the Word List on page 178 to identify the "speaker" in each sentence below.

Example: _______Incredulous_______ says, "I just don't believe it!"

1. _______________________ asks, "What if…?"

2. _______________________ explains "Let me make myself perfectly clear!"

3. _______________________ argues, "I will tell you why that's not true."

4. _______________________ informs, "Let me tell you what's what."

5. _______________________ says, "That's like a square peg in a round hole!"

6. _______________________ states, "Look at this from a variety of angles."

7. _______________________ states, "That is my opinion."

8. _______________________ commands, "Give up and go home!"

9. _______________________ pleads, "It's good for you."

10. _______________________ laughs, "How ridiculous!"

11. _______________________ exclaims, "That is the code I live by."

12. _______________________ says, "I give her the credit for doing all the hard work."

13. _______________________ states, "You can believe me."

14. _______________________ says, "I can do that from memory."

15. _______________________ asks, "What if you assume?"

**Speak It!** With a small group, create a TV talk-show interview. The host can interview a famous thinker, a scientist who has just made a discovery, or a politician who wants to change the world. Write your interview, practice it, and perform it for the class.
Use several vocabulary words from this unit.

**PART 1**

# Context Clues



## The Importance of Evidence:
# From Crime Scene to Court

**When a crime is committed, the people responsible must be brought to justice. The investigation begins at the crime scene, makes a stop at the crime lab, and if there is enough evidence, ends in a court of law.**

A person is missing. A bank is robbed. A murder is committed. Detectives are called in to begin the investigation. Painstakingly, they comb every square inch of the scene by searching, sifting, lifting fingerprints, and vacuuming fibers. They examine, measure, photograph, and record every detail. Then they seal the evidence in jars or bags, label it, and send it to the crime lab. Detectives must act in strict **compliance** with the laws by gathering and using evidence only in legal ways.

At the crime lab, **forensic** analysis of the evidence begins. Analysis is done through the use of chemicals, microscopes, X-rays, and other instruments and procedures. For example, hair found at a crime scene might be chemically tested to determine whether it comes from a victim or a suspect. Clothing particles found in a rug might be examined under a microscope and then matched with a suspect's clothing. Fingerprints, footprints, and tire tracks can be analyzed, or traced through databases.

Detectives use all this evidence, along with the testimony of witnesses, to help them identify the **culprit**. Nevertheless, sometimes the evidence and testimony aren't strong enough. Detectives want evidence that is more than **circumstantial** and just seemingly related to the crime. Sometimes, detectives keep a suspect under **surveillance** by keeping a constant watch on his or her activities and noting any suspicious behavior. Sometimes, this leads to the discovery of more direct evidence and the arrest of whoever **perpetrated** the crime.

When the court case begins, lawyers for the **prosecution** take over, using the evidence to build a case against the accused person. They will be challenged by lawyers for the defense, who will try to prove the innocence of the accused. These opposing lawyers may try to establish an **alibi** by showing that the accused wasn't at the crime scene when the crime was committed. They will try to discredit the testimony of witnesses or call evidence into question. In short, they will do anything legal that might prove **injurious** to the prosecution's case or the detective's work. In the end, however, only the jury can decide whether to convict or to **acquit** the accused person.

# Context Clues Strategy

## Look for How Something Is Done

**EXAMPLE:** The witness took her *oath* by swearing to tell the truth.

**CLUE:** This sentence explains the meaning of the word *oath* by telling how a person takes an oath in a court of law. The sentence makes it clear that the oath involves a promise, or solemn statement, about telling the truth.

Here is another strategy for using context clues to figure out the meaning of new words, such as *alibi* from the essay on page 182.

**Read** the sentence with the unknown word and some of the sentences around it.

*These opposing lawyers may try to establish an* **alibi** *by showing that the accused wasn't at the crime scene when the crime was committed.*

**Look** for context clues to the word's meaning. What clues to **How Something Is Done** do you find?

The sentence says that establishing an *alibi* involves showing that the accused person wasn't there when the crime was committed.

**Think** about the context clues and other information you may already know.

I have seen detective shows on television in which someone accused of a crime tries to provide an *alibi* to prove he or she could not have committed the crime during a certain time.

**Predict** a meaning for the word.

I think *alibi* means "proof that a person was somewhere else."

**Check** your Word Wisdom Dictionary to be sure of the meaning. Which of the meanings fits the context?

In this context, *alibi* means "a claim to have been somewhere else when a crime was committed."

**Practice the Strategy** Look at these two boldfaced words from the essay on page 182. Use the context clues strategy on page 183 to figure out the meaning of each word.

### compliance

📖 **Read** the sentence that uses the word *compliance* and some of the sentences around it.

🔍 **Look** for context clues to the word's meaning. What clues to **How Something Is Done** can you find?

_______________________________________________

💡 **Think** about the context clues. What other helpful information do you know?

_______________________________________________

➡️ **Predict** a meaning for the word *compliance*.

_______________________________________________

✔️ **Check** your Word Wisdom Dictionary to be sure of the meaning of the word *compliance*. Write the definition here.

_______________________________________________

### surveillance

📖 **Read** the sentence that uses the word *surveillance* and some of the sentences around it.

🔍 **Look** for context clues to the word's meaning. What clues to **How Something Is Done** can you find?

_______________________________________________

💡 **Think** about the context clues. What other helpful information do you know?

_______________________________________________

➡️ **Predict** a meaning for the word *surveillance*.

_______________________________________________

✔️ **Check** your Word Wisdom Dictionary to be sure of the meaning of the word *surveillance*. Write the definition here.

_______________________________________________

**Use Context Clues**  You have been introduced to three vocabulary words from the essay on page 182. Those words are checked off in the Word List. In the first column, write the remaining seven words from the Word List. In the second column, predict a meaning for each word using context clues. Then look up each word in the Word Wisdom Dictionary and write its definition in the third column.

| Vocabulary Word | Your Prediction | Dictionary Says |
|---|---|---|
| 1 | | |
| 2 | | |
| 3 | | |
| 4 | | |
| 5 | | |
| 6 | | |
| 7 | | |

**WORD LIST**
- compliance
- forensic
- culprit
- circumstantial
- surveillance
- perpetrate
- prosecution
- alibi
- injurious
- acquit

**Choose the Correct Words** Write the vocabulary word that completes each sentence in the paragraph. You may need to change one word's ending.

When the Salinas family's house was burglarized, nobody ever found the person who **1** _______________ the crime. The police had a theory about who the **2** _______________ was. They even mentioned the possibility of keeping someone under **3** _______________. Still, a lot of time passed, and no one was ever charged. Their suspect either had a great **4** _______________, or all the evidence against him was purely **5** _______________ and insufficient for a case.

**Write the Sentences** Write a sentence that uses all the words in each group. You may use the words in any order and change the endings of words.

**6** laboratory, forensic, evidence

_______________________________________________

_______________________________________________

**7** prosecution, witness, testify

_______________________________________________

_______________________________________________

**8** acquit, accused, person

_______________________________________________

_______________________________________________

**9** evidence, injurious, case

_______________________________________________

_______________________________________________

**10** officers, compliance, laws

_______________________________________________

_______________________________________________

**Connect the Words** Write the word from the Word List that goes with each clue.

**1** Let's keep an eye on him. ______________________

**2** I couldn't have done it! I was at home all night. ______________________

**3** We find the defendant not guilty. ______________________

**4** This evidence is NOT "beyond a shadow of a doubt." ______________________

**5** We have to do it this way. It's the law. ______________________

**6** She committed the crime. ______________________

**7** The scientific evidence solved the crime. ______________________

**8** That was very hurtful. ______________________

**9** The government accusers had a strong case. ______________________

**10** Catch the guilty person! ______________________

**Complete the Sentences** Complete each sentence.

**11** If you **perpetrate** a crime you could go to jail because ______________________

______________________

**12** We thought we could identify the **culprit** because ______________________

______________________

**13** The piece of fabric was considered **forensic** evidence because ______________________

______________________

**14** The **prosecution** did not succeed because ______________________

______________________

**15** The accused person's own testimony was **injurious** to his case because ______

______________________

**Write It!** Analyze the pros and cons of a career in law enforcement. Write a paragraph about what you might like and dislike about the job. Use several Part 1 vocabulary words.

# PART 2

# Latin Roots

*for Word Wisdom*

## Sheriffs and Constables:
# Officers of the Law

**Are the top law officers in your community elected or hired? Are they paid or unpaid? What powers and responsibilities do they have? To whom do they answer?**

Law enforcement has a clear, logical structure in some communities. It's a complex bureaucracy in others. For example, do you know the difference between a sheriff and a **constable**? A sheriff is elected as the main law enforcement officer. A sheriff's **jurisdiction** is the county that elected him or her. A sheriff carries out laws and **statutes,** serves warrants issued by judges, and generally preserves the peace. The warrants may involve petty theft, truancy, assault, **perjury,** or other offenses. He or she makes sure that **supplicants** appear in court. Sometimes a sheriff will determine the extent of damages someone has caused. Then that person can be required by law to make **restitution** by paying the owner of the property for the damage. The sheriff is often in charge of the county jail and its prisoners.

A constable, on the other hand, often has the same duties as a sheriff but less authority. Not all states have constables, but states that do usually elect them. Many constables are trained law enforcement officers, but others are untrained.

The position of constable was adopted from England, where the constables were equal to sheriffs in every way except training. In the United States, the responsibilities of constables vary greatly, from handling paperwork for judges to performing traffic and patrol duties. Some constables are not directly responsible to any governing body. Even though most constables are elected, it can be difficult to identify their **constituents**.

Some constables are more like business people than law officers. They collect money for the courts and are paid directly from these funds. Records are sometimes sketchy, nevertheless. A lack of records can provide opportunities for **duplicity** by allowing someone to steal the money. Good constables resist this temptation to steal. Some constables deputize people, give them badges, and send them out to collect money. In many places, a deputy needs to be twenty-one years of age and a resident of the state.

Constables are sometimes given the responsibility of arresting criminals and their **accomplices,** or helpers. If a person is suspected of **complicity** in a crime, he or she is likely to be arrested along with the criminal.

Constables help small or overworked police departments. They serve warrants and collect thousands of dollars in fines that would otherwise go unpaid. In this way, they help support the entire community. Constables in some areas handle tasks ranging from organizing neighborhood watch programs to directing traffic at accidents.

**Practice the Context Clues Strategy** Here are two of the
boldfaced words from the essay on page 188. Use the context clues
strategy you learned in Part 1 on page 183 to figure out the meanings
of these words.

## restitution

**Read** the sentence that uses the word *restitution* and some of the sentences
around it.

**Look** for context clues to the word's meaning. What clues showing **How
Something Is Done** can you find?

_______________________________________________

**Think** about the context clues. What other information do you know?

_______________________________________________

**Predict** a meaning for the word *restitution*.

_______________________________________________

**Check** your Word Wisdom Dictionary to be sure of the meaning of the
word *restitution*. Write the definition here.

_______________________________________________

## duplicity

**Read** the sentence that uses the word *duplicity* and some of the sentences
around it.

**Look** for context clues to the word's meaning. What clues showing **How
Something Is Done** can you find?

_______________________________________________

**Think** about the context clues. What other information do you know?

_______________________________________________

**Predict** a meaning for the word *duplicity*.

_______________________________________________

**Check** your Word Wisdom Dictionary to be sure of the meaning of the
word *duplicity*. Write the definition here.

_______________________________________________

Many English words have Latin roots. Knowing the meanings of roots can help you understand the meanings of many words. Some of the words you studied in Part 1 have Latin roots. Each root below is related to law and order.

Latin Root: **sta, stit**
meaning: to stand
English word: *circumstantial*
meaning: having a possible but not definite connection

Latin Root: **ple, pli, plic**
meaning: to fold
English word: *compliance*
meaning: in obedience to or agreement with

Latin Root: **jud, jur, jus**
meaning: right, law, to swear
English word: *injurious*
meaning: harmful

**WORD LIST**

- constable
- jurisdiction
- statute
- perjury
- supplicant
- restitution
- constituent
- duplicity
- accomplice
- complicity

**Categorize by Roots**  Find these roots in the Word List. Then write each word in the correct column. Add other words you know that come from the same Latin roots.

Latin Root: **sta, stit**

Latin Root: **ple, pli, plic**

Latin Root: **jud, jur, jus**

**Law and Order**

<table>
<tr><td>**Prefix**<br>com-</td><td>**Meaning**<br>with, together</td></tr>
</table>

**Example**

**com-** (with, together) **+ plic** (fold) **+ -ity** (noun) **=** **complicity**

**Use Roots and Prefixes**  Circle the root and any prefix you find in the boldfaced words below. Use context clues, roots, and prefixes to write the meaning of the word. Check your definitions in the dictionary.

**1** Because Mr. Thomas had supplied the getaway car, he was guilty of **complicity** in the robbery.

_______________________________________________

**2** The sincere and remorseful **supplicant** asked the judge for mercy.

_______________________________________________

**3** Are you aware of the **statute** that prevents you from driving on the beach?

_______________________________________________

**4** Dan decided to make **restitution** for the property he had damaged.

_______________________________________________

**5** The robber did not act alone; she had an **accomplice**.

_______________________________________________

**6** The senator is responsible to her **constituents** for her actions and positions.

_______________________________________________

**7** Malcolm said he was telling the truth, but Dylan suspected him of **duplicity**.

_______________________________________________

**8** The judge warned Candace that lying under oath is **perjury**.

_______________________________________________

**9** The **constable** attended to duties that the sheriff didn't have time for.

_______________________________________________

**10** The court could not rule on the case because it was outside its **jurisdiction**.

_______________________________________________

**WORD LIST**

constable

jurisdiction

statute

perjury

supplicant

restitution

constituent

duplicity

accomplice

complicity

**Find the Synonyms**  Write the word from the Word List that is a synonym for the underlined word or words in each sentence.

**1** The thief refused to give the name of his <u>partner in crime</u>.

_______________________________________________

**2** According to this state <u>law</u>, no arrest can be made in this case.

_______________________________________________

**3** Which court has the <u>legal authority</u> to rule on this case?

_______________________________________________

**4** The victim wanted <u>repayment</u> for the damage done to her property.

_______________________________________________

**5** Mrs. Parmenter could find no explanation for her daughter's <u>deceit</u>.

_______________________________________________

**Complete the Sentences**  Write the vocabulary word that completes each sentence.

**6** We asked the _______________________ to explain our town's laws.

**7** The compassionate judge could not refuse the request of the humble

_______________________.

**8** A _______________________ can take part in government by e-mailing his

or her opinions to an elected representative.

**9** Everyone thought she had been involved in the crime in some way, but no

one could prove her _______________________.

**10** The witness committed _______________________ by giving misleading

and false statements.

# Apply What You've Learned

**Answer the Questions** Use what you've learned about the boldfaced words to answer each question.

**1** Where would you be likely to find a **constable?** _______________

_____________________________________________

**2** When would someone be required to make **restitution?** _______________

_____________________________________________

**3** When would someone feel tempted to use **duplicity?** _______________

_____________________________________________

**4** What might a **supplicant** ask of a police officer who stopped him for speeding?

_____________________________________________

**5** Where would you find a town's **statutes?** _______________

_____________________________________________

**6** Why would a senator listen to his **constituents'** concerns? _______________

_____________________________________________

**7** What is the **jurisdiction** of a county sheriff? _______________

_____________________________________________

**8** What is the difference between lying to a friend and committing **perjury?**

_____________________________________________

**9** What might a thief's **accomplice** do? _______________

_____________________________________________

**10** How could doing nothing result in a person's **complicity** in a crime?

_____________________________________________

**Speak It!** Suppose you were running for class president. Prepare a two-minute speech explaining what new rules you would like to see at school or any rules you would like to see changed. Use as many words from the Part 2 Word List as you can.

# PART 3 Reference Skills

*for Word Wisdom*

## Small Claims Court:
# Seeking Justice

**What could you do if your new CD player fell apart and the store would not give you another one? What if your parents loaned some money to a neighbor, who now insists that she does not have to pay it back? Small claims court was established for these kinds of situations.**

Small claims court is an informal court that rarely has lawyers and never has a jury. Anyone who is eighteen or older can use this court to sue another person or a business. A parent or guardian can represent anyone younger than eighteen. You don't even have to be a citizen of the United States. In small claims court, you can sue only for money. That is, you cannot force another person to do anything except pay you money. The maximum amount of the payment is different in different states. It might be $3,000 in one state and $5,000 in another. To sue for more, you must use a different court.

In small claims court, people represent themselves. One person is the plaintiff, the person who is suing. The other person is the defendant, the person who is being sued. An **impartial** judge listens to both sides and objectively decides whether the defendant has caused any damages and is **liable** to pay for them. Defendants might insist that they are innocent, or they might explain **extenuating** circumstances that led to the problem. After considering both sides, the judge might announce a decision right then or days later. The judge might decide that the defendant is guilty of some kind of **infraction** and give this person an **ultimatum** to pay for the damages. However, if the judge does not believe the defendant is responsible for any damages, that defendant might be **exonerated**. Of course, all judges are human, so some are **lenient,** while others are strict, following the law to the letter.

Sometimes a defendant **retaliates** by filing a counterclaim against the plaintiff, suing the plaintiff for some kind of damages. This counterclaim can be filed at the same time as the original claim or within a few days of the judge's decision. The counterclaim, like the original claim, must not exceed the maximum amount for that state's small claims court.

Instead of going to small claims court, two people who have a dispute might try mediation. Many communities have dispute resolution centers. There, an arbitrator will try to **mediate** the conflict by helping both people listen to each other and find a way to solve the problem. Mediation allows people to **reconcile** their differences without suing each other. The people involved discuss possible solutions, choose one that they both can accept, and sign a binding agreement that they promise to follow.

When people interact, they are bound to have disagreements and disputes. Mediation and small claims court can help them settle these differences without resorting to trials and lawyers.

**Practice the Context Clues Strategy**   Here are two of the boldfaced words from the essay on page 194. Use the context clues strategy you learned in Part 1 on page 183 to figure out the meanings of these words.

## impartial

**Read** the sentence that uses the word *impartial* and some of the sentences around it.

**Look** for context clues to the word's meaning. What clues showing **How Something Is Done** can you find?

_______________________________________________

**Think** about the context clues. What other information do you know?

_______________________________________________

**Predict** a meaning for the word *impartial*.

_______________________________________________

**Check** your Word Wisdom Dictionary to be sure of the meaning of the word *impartial*. Write the definition here.

_______________________________________________

## mediate

**Read** the sentence that uses the word *mediate* and some of the sentences around it.

**Look** for context clues to the word's meaning. What clues showing **How Something Is Done** can you find?

_______________________________________________

**Think** about the context clues. What other information do you know?

_______________________________________________

**Predict** a meaning for the word *mediate*.

_______________________________________________

**Check** your Word Wisdom Dictionary to be sure of the meaning of the word *mediate*. Write the definition here.

_______________________________________________

# 🔒 Unlock the Meanings

**Word Origins** Large dictionaries usually include the etymology, or history, of a word. This is usually done by showing the earlier words and languages the word came from. This information is often enclosed in brackets at the end of an entry.

**le•ni•ent** /lē′ nē ənt/ *adj.* not harsh or strict; merciful. *The judge was very lenient in his sentences.* [from Latin *lenis,* soft.]

Many words about the law came into English from Latin. This is because Latin was once an international language shared by church and government officials and scholars.

**Find the Word Histories** Use a dictionary to find the source of each of these words. Write source words and their meanings. Then write a sentence to explain the connection between the source word and the modern word.

**1** exonerate ________________________________

________________________________

________________________________

**2** ultimatum ________________________________

________________________________

________________________________

**3** alibi ________________________________

________________________________

________________________________

________________________________

**4** mediate ________________________________

________________________________

________________________________

**5** constable ________________________________

________________________________

________________________________

**1.** Use context clues.

**2.** Look for a familiar root, prefix, or suffix.

**3.** If the context or a word part doesn't help, check the dictionary.

**WORD LIST**
impartial
liable
extenuating
infraction
ultimatum
exonerate
lenient
retaliate
mediate
reconcile

**Define the Words** Follow the steps above to write the meaning of each boldfaced word. Write 1, 2, or 3 to show which steps you used.

**1** There were **extenuating** circumstances that caused Ling's homework to be late.

_______________________________________________

**2** After Bo showed up late again, Mr. Brown gave him this **ultimatum:** "Get here on time, or don't come at all!"

_______________________________________________

**3** When Rob insulted Liam, Liam wanted to **retaliate** with an insult of his own.

_______________________________________________

**4** The jury didn't have enough evidence to convict, so it **exonerated** the man.

_______________________________________________

**5** Cheating is not only wrong but also an **infraction** of the school honor code.

_______________________________________________

**6** The criminal expected harsh punishment, but the judge was **lenient.**

_______________________________________________

**7** Because the two sides were so far apart in their thinking, the case was difficult to **mediate.**

_______________________________________________

**8** Judges cannot let their own opinions influence a case; they must be **impartial.**

_______________________________________________

**9** The driver of the car was **liable** for the damage that resulted from the accident.

_______________________________________________

**10** The court was able to **reconcile** the dispute between the neighbors.

_______________________________________________

# Process the Meanings

**WORD LIST**

impartial

liable

extenuating

infraction

ultimatum

exonerate

lenient

retaliate

mediate

reconcile

**Find the Antonyms**  Write the word from the Word List that is an antonym for the underlined word in each sentence. You may need to change the word's ending.

**1** The king was <u>merciless</u> in his response to the wrongdoing.

_______________________________________________

**2** The woman offered a <u>biased</u> view of the events that led up to the accident.

_______________________________________________

**3** Some townspeople hoped that the courts would <u>convict</u> Clara of the crime.

_______________________________________________

**4** The couple <u>argued</u> over their differences.

_______________________________________________

**Complete the Sentences**  Write the word from the Word List that completes each sentence. You may need to change the ending of a word.

**5** When Mom delivered her _______________________ about my grades, I knew I had to get serious about studying.

**6** When the team captain missed practice, the coach knew there must be _______________________ circumstances.

**7** Brad was usually calm, but when Katie insulted him, he wanted to _______________________ .

**8** Students with three _______________________ can be suspended from school.

**9** If you print that untrue statement, you might be found _______________________ for your actions.

**10** A trained negotiator was called in to _______________________ the dispute.

**Solve the Riddles** Write a word from the Word List for each clue.

**1** This is your last chance! Take it or leave it. ______________________

**2** I fight back when attacked! ______________________

**3** The scales of justice are balanced in my hands. ______________________

**4** I'm bigger than a lie but smaller than a crime. ______________________

**5** I will go easy on you. ______________________

**Demonstrate Word Knowledge** Answer each question or follow the directions.

**6** How would you help to **reconcile** differences between two friends?

______________________

______________________

**7** Write a newspaper headline that might appear when a celebrity is **exonerated**.

______________________

______________________

**8** Describe some **extenuating** circumstances that might explain why you were late for school.

______________________

______________________

**9** Name an action that would make you **liable**.

______________________

______________________

**10** How are *mediate* and *intercede* alike?

______________________

______________________

**Write It!** Write a dialogue between two people who are trying to reconcile some difference, such as which restaurant to go to. Use as many words from the Part 3 Word List as you can.

**PART 4**

# Review
*for Word Wisdom*

**Categorize by Parts of Speech** Determine whether each word in the Word List is a noun, a verb, or an adjective. Write the word in the correct column.

## WORD LIST

- compliance
- forensic
- culprit
- circumstantial
- surveillance
- perpetrate
- prosecution
- alibi
- injurious
- acquit
- constable
- jurisdiction
- statute
- perjury
- supplicant
- restitution
- constituent
- duplicity
- accomplice
- complicity
- impartial
- liable
- extenuating
- infraction
- ultimatum
- exonerate
- lenient
- retaliate
- mediate
- reconcile

| Nouns | Verbs | Adjectives |
|-------|-------|------------|
|       |       |            |

**Classify the Words**  Write the word from the Word List that completes each group.

**1** sneakiness, underhandedness, ________________________

**2** police officer, sheriff, ________________________

**3** criminal, wrongdoer, ________________________

**4** harmful, hurtful, ________________________

**5** excuse, explanation, ________________________

**6** fair, unbiased, ________________________

**7** fight back, counterattack, ________________________

**8** obedience, conformity, ________________________

**Choose the Correct Words**  Write the vocabulary word in parentheses that completes each sentence.

**9** The jury spent thirty hours deciding whether to convict or

________________________ the defendant. (acquit, mediate)

**10** The victim of the robbery demanded ________________________ for his

losses. (infraction, restitution)

**11** Although her car was used in the robbery, she denied any

________________________ in the crime. (complicity, jurisdiction)

**12** To be sure we understood our legal rights, we reread the

________________________. (statute, ultimatum)

**13** The house that belongs to the suspected criminal is being kept under

________________________. (jurisdiction, surveillance)

**14** A(n) ________________________ expert will be examining some of the

evidence that the detectives gathered. (forensic, extenuating)

**15** The evidence seemed to suggest that the thief had carried out the crime

with a(n) ________________________. (accomplice, alibi)

# Taking Vocabulary Tests

## TEST-TAKING STRATEGY

Some test takers spend too much time on the first item, or the first several items. A better strategy is to look over the whole test and do the easiest items first. This way you complete items you're likely to get right. Doing the easiest items first can also raise your confidence level and make the rest of the test appear less overwhelming.

### Sample:

Read the paragraph carefully. Then fill in the circle of the item that BEST completes the statement.

Justin knew he had messed 1
up again. If he was late one 2
more time, he would lose his 3
job. There was no question 4
about that outcome. His boss 5
had given him an **ultimatum**. 6

In line 6, the word *ultimatum* is best defined as

Ⓐ lecture
Ⓑ final warning
Ⓒ negative rating
Ⓓ punishment

**Practice Test**  Read each paragraph carefully. Then fill in the circle of the item that BEST completes the statement.

**1**  Trish had seen a group of 1
girls being mean to Lindsey. 2
Trish could have stopped it, 3
but she didn't. Was she 4
guilty of **complicity**? 5

In line 5, *complicity* is best defined as

Ⓐ partial involvement in wrongdoing
Ⓑ mistreatment of other people
Ⓒ giving into peer pressure
Ⓓ taking the lead in wrongdoing

**2**  The evidence suggested 1
that Mandy had been at the 2
house on the night it was 3
robbed. That didn't prove 4
she had any part in it. The 5
evidence was **circumstantial**. 6

In line 6, *circumstantial* is best defined as

Ⓐ perhaps, but not definitely related
Ⓑ definitely related
Ⓒ impossible to prove
Ⓓ impossible to disprove

**3**  The principal told Zach 1
that the **infraction** was not 2
serious. She warned, how- 3
ever, that future violations 4
would become part of his 5
permanent school record. 6

In line 2, *infraction* is best defined as

Ⓐ criminal action
Ⓑ minor violation
Ⓒ escape from prison
Ⓓ vandalism of school property

**4**  The defendant was 1
innocent, but few people 2
realized that. When one of 3
the witnesses committed 4
**perjury**, the defendant 5
gave up hope of receiving 6
a "not guilty" verdict. 7

In line 5, *perjury* is best defined as

Ⓐ proof that a person is guilty
Ⓑ proof that a person is innocent
Ⓒ an act of reversing prior testimony
Ⓓ an act of lying under oath

**5**  For a crime like this, the 1
judge usually passed out 2
harsh sentences. This time 3
was different, however. 4
The sentence was **lenient**, 5
perhaps because the 6
criminal had no prior 7
record. 8

In line 5, *lenient* is best defined as

Ⓐ harsh
Ⓑ unusual
Ⓒ appropriate
Ⓓ merciful

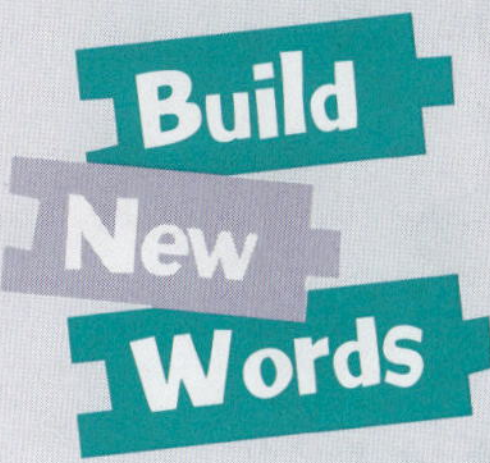

**Build New Words**

**Add Suffixes** Some words add the endings *-ous*, *-ory*, or *-al* to form adjectives or other parts of speech. Another spelling change is sometimes involved. For example, the word *injury* changes to *injurious* by first changing the *y* to *i* and then adding *-ous*. In the chart below, add the suffix *-ous*, *-ory*, or *-al* to make new words. Use your dictionary to find the new words and their spellings. Then use the new word in a sentence.

| Word | + Suffix | = New Word | Sentence |
|---|---|---|---|
| duplicity | | | |
| perjury | | | |
| acquit | | | |
| retaliate | | | |
| statute | | | |

**Speak It!** Watch a television program that includes a courtroom trial. It can be a real trial or a fictional one. Give an oral report to the class explaining who was accused of a crime, what evidence there was, and what the jury decided. Use as many words from this unit as you can.

# W!rd Wisdom Dictionary



**PRONUNCIATION KEY**

| | |
|---|---|
| /ă/ | pat |
| /ā/ | pay |
| /â/ | care |
| /ä/ | father |
| /är/ | far |
| /ĕ/ | pet |
| /ē/ | be |
| /ĭ/ | pit |
| /ī/ | pie |
| /îr/ | pier |
| /ŏ/ | mop |
| /ō/ | toe |
| /ô/ | paw, for |
| /oi/ | noise |
| /ou/ | out |
| /o͝o/ | look |
| /o͞o/ | boot |
| /ŭ/ | cut |
| /ûr/ | urge |
| /th/ | thin |
| /th/ | this |
| /hw/ | what |
| /zh/ | vision |
| /ə/ | about |
| | item |
| | pencil |
| | gallop |
| | circus |
| /ər/ | butter |

## A

**ab•di•cate** /ăb′ dĭ kāt′/ *v.* **ab•di•cat•ed, ab•di•cat•ing, ab•di•cates.** to officially give up or renounce a high office or responsibility. *The king will abdicate the throne.*

**ab•di•ca•tion** /ăb′ dĭ kā′ shən/ *n.* the renouncement of a high office or responsibility. *Her abdication from the company left the boss in a panic.*

**ab•er•ra•tion** /ăb′ ə rā′ shən/ *n.* a departure from the normal or typical. *Jeremy's recent behavior is a definite aberration.*

**ab•o•li•tion•ist** /ăb′ ə lĭsh′ ə nĭst/ *n.* a person who works to end a law or custom. *Abolitionists fought hard to end slavery.*

**ac•cess¹** /ăk′ sĕs/ *n.* the right to enter or use. *We were able to gain access to the stadium's private club.*

**ac•cess²** /ăk′ sĕs/ *v.* **ac•cessed, ac•cess•ing, ac•cess•es.** to obtain entry or use. *You can access the file on my computer.*

**ac•com•plice** /ə kŏm′ plĭs/ *n.* a partner in doing something wrong or illegal. *The police caught the robber and his accomplice.*

**ac•crue¹** /ə kro͞o′/ *v.* **ac•crued, ac•cru•ing, ac•crues.** to accumulate something over a period of time. *Our debate team accrued the most points.* —**ac•crue•ment** *n.*

**ac•crue²** /ə kro͞o′/ *v.* **ac•crued, ac•cru•ing, ac•crues.** to increase in amount or value. *Your money will accrue interest in the bank.* —**ac•crue•ment** *n.*

**ac•quit** /ə kwĭt′/ *v.* **ac•quit•ted, ac•quit•ting, ac•quits.** to free or clear from a legal accusation of wrongdoing. *The accused man was acquitted of the crime.*

**ac•quit•tal** /ə kwĭt′ l/ *n.* judgement by a court that clears a defendant of wrongdoing. *The defendant was relieved to hear of his acquittal.*

**ad•ver•sar•y** /ăd′ vər sĕr′ ē/ *n., pl.* **ad•ver•sar•ies.** an opponent; an enemy. *The football teams were adversaries.*

**ad•ver•si•ty** /ăd vûr′ sĭ tē/ *n., pl.* **ad•ver•si•ties.** misfortune; hardship. *The hurricane victims suffered much adversity.*

**af•fect¹** /ə fĕkt′/ *v.* **af•fect•ed, af•fect•ing, af•fects.** to influence or cause something or someone to change. *The storm will affect our travel plans.*

**af•fect²** /ə fĕkt′/ *v.* **af•fect•ed, af•fect•ing, af•fects.** to move someone emotionally. *Her kind actions affected everyone.*

**af•fil•i•ate[1]** /ə fĭl′ ē ĭt/ *n.* an individual or organization joined with a larger group. *The community college is an affiliate of the state university.*

**af•fil•i•ate[2]** /ə fĭl′ ē āt/ *v.* **af•fil•i•at•ed, af•fil•i•at•ing, af•fil•i•ates.** to join a group of common interest. *Our chess club plans to affiliate with a national network of chess lovers.*

**af•fir•ma•tive[1]** /ə fûr′ mə tĭv/ *adj.* positive. *Her affirmative outlook is difficult to sway.* —**af•fir•ma•tive•ly** *adv.*

**af•fir•ma•tive[2]** /ə fûr′ mə tĭv/ *adj.* stating that something is true. *The teacher gave an affirmative nod after Josh's answer.* —**af•fir•ma•tive•ly** *adv.*

**af•fir•ma•tive[3]** /ə fûr′ mə tĭv/ *n.* a statement of agreement. *We replied in the affirmative.*

**al•i•bi[1]** /ăl′ ə bī/ *n., pl.* **al•i•bis.** a claim to have been somewhere else when a crime was committed. *An alibi clears him of any guilt.*

**al•i•bi[2]** /ăl′ ə bī/ *n. informal, pl.* **al•i•bis.** an excuse. *My brother has an alibi for everything.*

**al•lo•cate** /ăl′ ə kāt/ *v.* **al•lo•cat•ed, al•lo•cat•ing, al•lo•cates.** to set aside for a certain purpose. *We allocate some of our savings for vacation.* —**al•lo•ca•ble** *adj.* —**al•lo•ca•tion** *n.*

**al•ti•tude** /ăl′ tĭ tōōd′ *or* ăl′ tĭ tyōōd′/ *n.* the distance above a set limit, such as sea level or the earth's surface. *Breathing becomes more difficult at a high altitude.* —**al•ti•tu•di•nal** *adj.*

**am•big•u•ous** /ăm bĭg′ yōō əs/ *adj.* unclear. *We were confused by the ambiguous answer.* —**am•big•u•ous•ly** *adv.* —**am•bi•gu•i•ty** *n.*

**am•i•ca•ble** /ăm′ ĭ kə bəl/ *adj.* friendly. *They settled their argument in an amicable way.* —**am•i•ca•bly** *adv.* —**am•i•ca•bil•i•ty** *n.* —**am•i•ca•ble•ness** *n.*

**a•nach•ro•nism** /ə năk′ rə nĭz′ əm/ *n.* something placed out of its historical time. *A covered wagon is an anachronism on today's modern highways.*

**an•a•lyze** /ăn′ ə līz′/ *v.* **an•a•lyzed, an•a•lyz•ing, an•a•lyz•es.** to study for the purpose of drawing conclusions. *We need to analyze why our team lost the hockey game.* —**an•a•lyz•a•ble** *adj.* —**an•a•ly•za•tion** *n.* —**an•a•lyz•er** *n.*

**an•ti•quat•ed** /ăn′ tĭ kwā′ tĭd/ *adj.* too old to be useful or in style. *The phonograph uses antiquated technology.* —**an•ti•quat•ed•ness** *n.*

**ap•por•tion** /ə pôr′ shən *or* ə pōr′ shən/ *v.* **ap•por•tioned, ap•por•tion•ing, ap•por•tions.** to divide up. *The camp counselor apportioned the pizzas fairly.*

**ap•prise** /ə prīz′/ *v.* to inform. *We will apprise the custodian of the leaky faucet.*

**as•so•nance** /ăs′ ə nəns/ *n.* the similarity of sounds, especially vowel sounds. *"He spoke to the folks" is an example of assonance.* —**as•so•nant** *adj., n.*

**at•trib•ute[1]** /ə trĭb′ yōōt/ *v.* **at•trib•ut•ed, at•trib•ut•ing, at•trib•utes.** to relate to a particular cause or source. *To what do you attribute your good grades in math?* —**at•trib•ut•a•ble** *adj.* —**at•tri•bu•tion** *n.*

**at•trib•ute[2]** /ăt′ rə byōōt′/ *n.* a quality or characteristic associated with a specific person or thing. *She has many positive attributes.*

**a•ver•sion** /ə vûr′ zhən *or* ə vûr′ shən/ *n.* a strong dislike. *The baby has an aversion to carrots.*

---

**B**

**ban•ish** /băn′ ĭsh/ *v.* **ban•ished, ban•ish•ing, ban•ish•es.** to send or drive away from a country or place. *Napoleon was banished to the island of St. Helena in 1815.*

**ban•ish•ment** /băn′ ĭsh mənt/ *n.* the act or state of being driven away from a country or place. *He finally returned home after twenty years of banishment.*

**ba•rom•e•ter** /bə rŏm′ ĭ tər/ *n.* an instrument that measures atmospheric pressure. *The barometer indicates a weather change.*
—**bar•o•met•ric** /băr′ ə mĕt′ rĭk/ *adj.*
—**bar•o•met•ri•cal** *adj.*
—**bar•o•met•ri•cal•ly** *adv.*
—**ba•rom•e•try** *n.*

**be•nev•o•lent** /bə nĕv′ ə lənt/ *adj.* kind. *The family's illness brought about many benevolent acts by their neighbors.*
—**be•nev•o•lent•ly** *adv.*

**blare[1]** /blâr/ *n.* a loud, harsh sound. *The blare of the horns interrupted our conversation.*

**blare[2]** /blâr/ *v.* **blared, blar•ing, blares.** to make a loud, harsh sound. *Impatient drivers blare their horns in traffic.*

## C

**ca•coph•o•ny** /kə kŏf′ ə nē/ *n., pl.* **ca•coph•o•nies.** a harsh or unpleasant sound. *The cacophony of screaming fans jangled our nerves.*

**ca•per[1]** /kā′ pər/ *v.* **ca•pered, ca•per•ing, ca•pers.** to leap or jump around playfully. *The happy children caper in the park.*

**ca•per[2]** /kā′ pər/ *n.* a playful leap. *Our cat's capers are fun to watch.*

**ca•per[3]** /kā′ pər/ *n.* a playful prank. *The innocent caper made us laugh.*

**cease** /sēs/ *v.* **ceased, ceas•ing, ceas•es.** to end; to stop. *We ceased talking when the conductor walked onstage.*

**chron•ic** /krŏn′ ĭk/ *adj.* lasting for a long time. *Our dog suffers from a chronic skin problem.* —**chron•i•cal•ly** *adv.*

**chron•i•cle[1]** /krŏn′ ĭ kəl/ *n.* a record of historic events presented in time order. *Public television presented a chronicle of jazz from its beginnings.*

**chron•i•cle[2]** /krŏn′ ĭ kəl/ *v.* **chron•i•cled, chron•i•cling, chron•i•cles.** to record historic events in time order. *The explorers chronicled their trip down the river.*
—**chron•i•cler** *n.*

**chron•o•log•i•cal** /krŏn′ ə lŏj′ ĭ kəl *or* krō′ nə lŏj′ ĭ kəl/ *adj.* listed in order of time. *The history book explained events in chronological order.*
—**chron•o•log•i•cal•ly** *adv.*

**cir•cum•stan•tial** /sûr′ kəm stăn′ shəl/ *adj.* related to an event that is connected to or affects another event or condition. *The evidence against her was only circumstantial.* —**cir•cum•stan•tial•ly** *adv.*

**co•hab•it** /kō hăb′ ĭt/ *v.* **co•hab•it•ed, co•hab•it•ing, co•hab•its.** to live together. *Animals in the forest usually cohabit in peace.* —**co•hab•i•tant** *n.*
—**co•hab•i•ta•tion** *n.*

**com•pel** /kəm pĕl′/ *v.* **com•pelled, com•pel•ling, com•pels.** to force or drive. *The flood might compel us to leave our home.* —**com•pel•la•ble** *adj.*
—**com•pel•la•bly** *adv.* —**com•pel•ler** *n.*

**com•pel•ling** /kəm pĕl′ ĭng/ *adj.* persuasive; forceful. *Your argument for saving the trees is a compelling one.*
—**com•pel•ling•ly** *adv.*

**com•pla•cent** /kəm plā′ sənt/ *adj.* self-satisfied; unconcerned. *The winner's complacent smile annoyed his opponents.* —**com•pla•cent•ly** *adv.*

**com•pli•ance** /kəm plī′ əns/ *n.* conforming to or agreeing with laws or rules. *Our principal expects compliance with all school rules.*

**com•plic•i•ty** /kəm plĭs′ ĭ tē/ *n., pl.* **com•plic•i•ties.** involvement in a crime or wrong action. *Richard denied complicity in the theft.*

**con•form** /kən fôrm′/ *v.* **con•formed, con•form•ing, con•forms.** to act in accord with laws or popular customs. *Members must conform to the club's rules.*
—**con•form•er** *n.* —**con•form•ist** *n.*

**con•found** /kən found′ *or* kŏn found′/ *v.* **con•found•ed, con•found•ing, con•founds.** to puzzle; to bewilder. *The teacher's decision to give another test confounds us.* —**con•found•er** *n.*

<br>

| PRONUNCIATION KEY | |
|---|---|
| /ă/ | pat |
| /ā/ | pay |
| /â/ | care |
| /ä/ | father |
| /är/ | far |
| /ĕ/ | pet |
| /ē/ | be |
| /ĭ/ | pit |
| /ī/ | pie |
| /îr/ | pier |
| /ŏ/ | mop |
| /ō/ | toe |
| /ô/ | paw, for |
| /oi/ | noise |
| /ou/ | out |
| /ŏŏ/ | look |
| /ōō/ | boot |
| /ŭ/ | cut |
| /ûr/ | urge |
| /th/ | thin |
| /th/ | this |
| /hw/ | what |
| /zh/ | vision |
| /ə/ | about |
| | item |
| | pencil |
| | gallop |
| | circus |
| /ər/ | butter |

**con•fuse** /kən fyo͞oz′/ *v.* **con•fused, con•fus•ing, con•fus•es.** to mix up; to baffle. *The directions through the park confused me.* —**con•fus•ing•ly** *adv.*

**con•fused** /kən fyo͞ozd′/ *adj.* baffled. *Jimmy looked confused trying to figure out the answer.* —**con•fus•ed•ness** *n.*

**con•fus•ed•ly** /kən fyo͞o′ zĭd lē/ *adv.* acting in a confused or puzzled way. *The old man confusedly searched for his gloves.*

**con•jec•ture**[1] /kən jĕk′ chər/ *n.* a guess based on partial information. *A detective makes many conjectures before solving a case.*

**con•jec•ture**[2] /kən jĕk′ chər/ *v.* **con•jec•tured, con•jec•tur•ing, con•jec•tures.** to make a guess based on partial information. *Based on her patient's symptoms, the doctor conjectured a diagnosis.*

**con•sol•i•date** /kən sŏl′ ĭ dāt′/ *v.* **con•sol•i•dat•ed, con•sol•i•dat•ing, con•sol•i•dates.** to combine into one. *Companies consolidate their operations to save money.* —**con•sol•i•da•tion** *n.* —**con•sol•i•da•tor** *n.*

**con•so•nant**[1] /kŏn′ sə nənt/ *n.* a letter that represents a consonant sound. *How many consonants are in your name?*

**con•so•nant**[2] /kŏn′ sə nənt/ *n.* a speech sound made by a partial or complete blocking of the breath. *The sounds of letters like* b, f, *and* p *are consonant sounds.*

**con•sta•ble** /kŏn′ stə bəl *or* kŭn′ stə bəl/ *n.* a public officer of lower rank than a sheriff. *The constable questioned the suspect.*

**con•stit•u•ent** /kən stĭch′ o͞o ənt/ *n.* a person who is represented by an elected official. *The senator listens carefully to her constituents.*

**con•tend** /kən tĕnd′/ *v.* **con•tend•ed, con•tend•ing, con•tends.** to compete. *Our debate team contended for first place in the competition.* —**con•tend•er** *n.*

**con•tro•ver•sial** /kŏn′ trə vûr′ shəl *or* kŏn′ trə vûr′ sē əl/ *adj.* causing a disagreement. *I avoid controversial topics when talking with people I don't know well.* —**con•tro•ver•sial•ly** *adv.* —**con•tro•ver•sial•ist** *n.* —**con•tro•ver•sy** *n.*

**con•ver•sion** /kən vûr′ zhən/ *n.* the act or state of being changed into another form, substance, or thing. *The conversion of ice into water occurs at 32 degrees Fahrenheit.*

**con•vert** /kən vûrt′/ *v.* **con•vert•ed, con•vert•ing, con•verts.** to change into another form, substance, or thing. *Solar panels convert the sun's energy into electricity.*

**con•vey** /kən vā′/ *v.* **con•veyed, con•vey•ing, con•veys.** to carry; to transport. *Planes convey mail to faraway cities.* —**con•vey•a•ble** *adj.*

**co•pi•ous** /kō′ pē əs/ *adj.* plentiful. *The farmer was pleased with his copious harvest.* —**co•pi•ous•ly** *adv.* —**co•pi•ous•ness** *n.*

**coy**[1] /koi/ *adj.* **coy•er, coy•est.** shy, sometimes avoiding social situations. *Allison is coy when meeting new people.* —**coy•ly** *adv.* —**coy•ness** *n.*

**coy**[2] /koi/ *adj.* **coy•er, coy•est.** pretending to be shy, sometimes in a playful manner. *The coy young girl finally agreed to show us her drawing.* —**coy•ly** *adv.* —**coy•ness** *n.*

**cre•dence** /krēd′ ns/ *n.* acceptance as true; a belief. *My mother gives little credence to my brother's wild tales.*

**cred•i•ble** /krĕd′ ə bəl/ *adj.* believable. *His excuse is credible.* —**cred•i•bly** *adv.* —**cred•i•bil•i•ty** *n.* —**cred•i•ble•ness** *n.*

**creed** /krēd/ *n.* a statement of belief; a set of principles. *My creed is to think before I act.*

**cul•prit** /kŭl′ prĭt/ *n.* a person guilty of a fault or crime. *We will catch the culprit who took our shoes during gym class.*

**cur•tail** /kər tāl′/ *v.* **cur•tailed, cur•tail•ing, cur•tails.** to cut short; to reduce. *We try to curtail our food expenses.* —**cur•tail•ment** *n.*

**cyn•i•cal** /sĭn′ ĭ kəl/ *adj.* negatively believing that people only do things for selfish reasons. *Jason's cynical attitude offends his friends.* —**cyn•i•cal•ly** *adv.* —**cyn•ic** *n.*

**D**

**daw·dle** /dôd′ l/ *v.* **daw·dled, daw·dling, daw·dles.** to waste time; to move slowly. *Jeremy always dawdles when it's time to study for a test.* —**daw·dling·ly** *adv.* —**daw·dler** *n.*

**dec·i·mate** /dĕs′ ə māt′/ *v.* **dec·i·mat·ed, dec·i·mat·ing, dec·i·mates.** to destroy a great number of. *Tornadoes decimate everything in their path.* —**dec·i·ma·tion** *n.*

**de·co·rum** /dĭ kôr′ əm *or* dĭ kōr′ əm/ *n.* appropriateness of behavior or conduct. *Our parents taught us to act with decorum at all times.*

**de·crep·it** /dĭ krĕp′ ĭt/ *adj.* broken down; in bad condition. *The decrepit building was torn down.* —**de·crep·it·ly** *adv.*

**deem** /dēm/ *v.* **deemed, deem·ing, deems.** to judge. *The nurse deemed it necessary to check the patient's temperature.*

**de·vi·ate** /dē′ vē āt′/ *v.* **de·vi·at·ed, de·vi·at·ing, de·vi·ates.** to turn aside or away from. *We must not deviate from our plans.* —**de·vi·a·tor** *n.*

**de·vi·ous** /dē′ vē əs/ *adj.* insincere, under-handed as to motives. *Miranda has a devious plan for leaving school early.* —**de·vi·ous·ly** *adv.* —**de·vi·ous·ness** *n.*

**dis·cern** /dĭ sûrn′ *or* dĭ zûrn′/ *v.* **dis·cerned, dis·cern·ing, dis·cerns.** to perceive or detect. *Mr. Nash always discerns what his students are up to.* —**dis·cern·i·ble** *adj.* —**dis·cern·i·bly** *adv.*

**dis·cred·it** /dĭs krĕd′ ĭt/ *v.* **dis·cred·it·ed, dis·cred·it·ing, dis·cred·its.** to cast doubt on someone or something. *Tom tried to discredit the test because he failed it.*

**dis·place** /dĭs plās′/ *v.* **dis·placed, dis·plac·ing, dis·plac·es.** to change the place of. *Forest fires displace wildlife.*

**dis·placed** /dĭs plāst′/ *adj.* forced out of a place. *Thousands of displaced people returned to their homeland after the war.*

**dis·pro·por·tion·ate** /dĭs′ prə pôr′ shə nĭt/ *adj.* not in correct relation or balance. *The teacher gave a disproportionate number of low grades.* —**dis·pro·por·tion·ate·ly** *adv.* —**dis·pro·por·tion·ate·ness** *n.*

**dis·so·nance** /dĭs′ ə nəns/ *n.* a harsh combination of sounds. *The dissonance of protesting voices surrounded us.* —**dis·so·nant** *adj.*

**dis·turb** /dĭ stûrb′/ *v.* **dis·turbed, dis·turb·ing, dis·turbs.** to distract or interrupt. *Please don't disturb me while I do my homework.* —**dis·turb·ing·ly** *adv.* —**dis·turb·er** *n.*

**di·ver·sion** /dĭ vûr′ zhən *or* dĭ vûr′ zhən/ *n.* something that acts as a distraction. *The funny movie was a good diversion from his bad day.*

**di·vert**[1] /dĭ vûrt′ *or* dĭ vûrt′/ *v.* **di·vert·ed, di·vert·ing, di·verts.** to change the path of. *They plan to divert the traffic from this road during construction.* —**di·vert·ing·ly** *adv.* —**di·vert·er** *n.*

**di·vert**[2] /dĭ vûrt′ *or* dĭ vûrt′/ *v.* **di·vert·ed, di·vert·ing, di·verts.** to distract; to take attention from. *The ringing telephone diverted Lisa's attention from reading.* —**di·vert·ing·ly** *adv.* —**di·vert·er** *n.*

**du·plic·i·tous** /dōō plĭs′ ĭ təs *or* dyōō plĭs′ ĭ təs/ *adj.* marked by deliberately misleading or deceitful behavior. *Her duplicitous behavior made her untrustworthy.*

**du·plic·i·ty** /dōō plĭs′ ĭ tē *or* dyōō plĭs′ ĭ tē/ *n., pl.* **du·plic·i·ties.** deliberate misleading; deceit. *I was punished for my duplicity.*

**dwin·dle** /dwĭn′ dl/ *v.* **dwin·dled, dwin·dling, dwin·dles.** to decrease little by little. *The heavy rain dwindled to a gentle shower.*

**dy·nam·ic** /dĭ năm′ ĭk/ *adj.* full of life or force. *The class president has a dynamic personality.* —**dy·nam·i·cal·ly** *adv.*

**E**

**ec·cen·tric**[1] /ĭk sĕn′ trĭk *or* ĕk sĕn′ trĭk/ *adj.* having a strange appearance or behavior. *The eccentric man wore socks and shoes that did not match.* —**ec·cen·tri·cal·ly** *adv.*

---

**PRONUNCIATION KEY**

| | |
|---|---|
| /ă/ | pat |
| /ā/ | pay |
| /â/ | care |
| /ä/ | father |
| /är/ | far |
| /ĕ/ | pet |
| /ē/ | be |
| /ĭ/ | pit |
| /ī/ | pie |
| /îr/ | pier |
| /ŏ/ | mop |
| /ō/ | toe |
| /ô/ | paw, for |
| /oi/ | noise |
| /ou/ | out |
| /ŏŏ/ | look |
| /ōō/ | boot |
| /ŭ/ | cut |
| /ûr/ | urge |
| /th/ | thin |
| /th/ | this |
| /hw/ | what |
| /zh/ | vision |
| /ə/ | about |
| | item |
| | pencil |
| | gallop |
| | circus |
| /ər/ | butter |

**ec•cen•tric**[2] /ĭk sĕn′ trĭk *or* ĕk sĕn′ trĭk/ *n.* a person whose behavior is considered unconventional. *The artist was considered an eccentric.* —**ec•cen•tri•cal•ly** *adv.*

**e•dict** /ē′ dĭkt′/ *n.* a proclamation or official command from someone in authority. *The king's edict required everyone to pay a tax.*

**e•lu•ci•date** /ĭ lōō′ sĭ dāt′/ *v.* **e•lu•ci•dat•ed, e•lu•ci•dat•ing, e•lu•ci•dates.** to clarify; to explain. *Will you please elucidate why we have to go to bed so early?* —**e•lu•ci•da•tive** *adj.* —**e•lu•ci•da•tion** *n.* —**e•lu•ci•da•tor** *n.*

**e•man•ci•pa•tion** /ĭ măn′ sə pā′ shən/ *n.* the act of freeing or liberating. *President Lincoln proclaimed the emancipation of the slaves.*

**en•er•gize** /ĕn′ ər jīz′/ *v.* **en•er•gized, en•er•giz•ing, en•er•giz•es.** to activate; to fill with energy. *Exercise helps to energize many people.* —**en•er•giz•er** *n.*

**en•sue** /ĕn sōō′/ *v.* **en•sued, en•su•ing, en•sues.** to follow as a result. *When the water pipe broke, a flood ensued.*

**en•voy** /ĕn′ voi′ *or* ŏn′ voi′/ *n.* a representative; a messenger. *The president sent an envoy because he couldn't go himself.*

**ep•och** /ĕp′ ək *or* ē′ pŏk′/ *n.* a period of time associated with important events or changes. *We live in an epoch of political upheaval.*

**e•qui•dis•tant** /ē′ kwĭ dĭs′ tənt *or* ĕk′ wĭ dĭs′ tənt/ *adj.* at the same distance. *The bushes are equidistant from the front door.* —**e•qui•dis•tant•ly** *adv.* —**e•qui•dis•tance** *n.*

**er•rant** /ĕr′ ənt/ *adj.* straying from what is proper. *Her errant behavior got her in trouble with her parents.* —**er•rant•ly** *adv.* —**er•rant** *n.*

**er•rat•ic** /ĭ răt′ ĭk/ *adj.* unpredictable; inconsistent. *Julian has erratic study habits.* —**er•rat•i•cal•ly** *adv.*

**er•ro•ne•ous** /ĭ rō′ nē əs/ *adj.* incorrect; mistaken. *The candidate admitted that he had made several erroneous statements.* —**er•ro•ne•ous•ly** *adv.* —**er•ro•ne•ous•ness** *n.*

**eth•i•cal** /ĕth′ ĭ kəl/ *adj.* morally upright; honest. *My grandfather was an ethical businessman.* —**eth•i•cal•ly** *adv.* —**eth•i•cal•ness** *n.*

**eth•nic** /ĕth′ nĭk/ *adj.* pertaining to a particular cultural, racial, religious, or national group. *Many different ethnic groups meet at the United Nations.* —**eth•ni•cal•ly** *adv.*

**ex•em•pla•ry** /ĭg zĕm′ plə rē/ *adj.* ideal; setting a good example. *Joe's actions are usually exemplary.* —**ex•em•plar•i•ly** *adv.*

**ex•hort** /ĭg zôrt′/ *v.* **ex•hort•ed, ex•hort•ing, ex•horts.** to encourage strongly. *The officer exhorted the troops to hold their ground.* —**ex•hort•er** *n.*

**ex•hor•ta•tion** /ĕg′ zôr tā′ shən *or* ĕk′ sôr tā′ shən/ *n.* the instance of strong encouragement. *Without the exhortation of his family, Mike may never have discovered his love for acting.*

**ex•on•er•ate** /ĭg zŏn′ ə rāt′/ *v.* **ex•on•er•at•ed, ex•on•er•at•ing, ex•on•er•ates.** to free from blame. *The witnesses to the accident seemed to exonerate the boy.* —**ex•on•er•a•tive** *adj.* —**ex•on•er•a•tion** *n.*

**ex•pe•dite** /ĕk′ spĭ dīt′/ *v.* **ex•pe•dit•ed, ex•pe•dit•ing, ex•pe•dites.** to get something done faster. *Michael has to expedite his research for the paper.* —**ex•pe•dit•er** *or* **ex•pe•di•tor** *n.*

**ex•pound** /ĭk spound′/ *v.* **ex•pound•ed, ex•pound•ing, ex•pounds.** to explain something in detail. *The instructor will expound on the rules for safe driving.* —**ex•pound•er** *n.*

**ex•tent** /ĭk stĕnt′/ *n.* degree or scope. *To some extent, I always knew I would be a teacher.*

**ex•ten•u•ate** /ĭk stĕn′ yōō āt′/ *v.* **ex•ten•u•at•ed, ex•ten•u•at•ing, ex•ten•u•ates.** to excuse partly. *Tom's circumstances extenuate his recent behavior.* —**ex•ten•u•a•tive** *adj.* —**ex•ten•u•a•to•ry** *adj.*

**ex•ten•u•at•ing** /ĭk stĕn′ yōō ā′ tĭng/ *adj.* lessening the seriousness by providing a partial excuse. *There were extenuating circumstances that caused us to be late.*

**ex•tro•vert** /ĕk′ strə vûrt′/ *n.* a person who loves social activity and being with others. *The extrovert was the life of the party.* —**ex•tro•vert•ed** *adj.*

**ex•u•ber•ant** /ĭg zōō′ bər ənt/ *adj.* full of boundless enthusiasm or joy. *The exuberant boys cheered for their school's soccer team.* —**ex•u•ber•ant•ly** *adv.*

## F

**fac•ile**[1] /făs′ əl/ *adj.* easy. *The athlete lifted the weight in a facile manner.* —**fac•ile•ly** *adv.* —**fac•ile•ness** *n.*

**fac•ile**[2] /făs′ əl/ *adj.* speaking with ease but without careful thought. *The facile student gave a quick answer to the question.* —**fac•ile•ly** *adv.* —**fac•ile•ness** *n.*

**fac•tor** /făk′ tər/ *n.* a condition contributing to a particular result. *The quarterback's injury was a factor in his team's loss.*

**fat•u•ous** /făch′ ōō əs/ *adj.* foolish; silly. *The clown had a fatuous smile on his face.* —**fat•u•ous•ly** *adv.* —**fat•u•ous•ness** *n.*

**fe•lic•i•tous** /fĭ lĭs′ ĭ təs/ *adj.* appropriate; suitable. *The cold weather was felicitous for the ice-skating party.* —**fe•lic•i•tous•ly** *adv.* —**fe•lic•i•tous•ness** *n.*

**fem•i•nist** /fĕm′ ə nĭst/ *n.* a person who works for equal rights for women. *Feminists fought for voting rights for women.*

**fer•vent** /fûr′ vənt/ *adj.* showing great emotion or belief. *Our students have a fervent desire to do something good for the community.* —**fer•vent•ly** *adv.*

**flam•boy•ant** /flăm boi′ ənt/ *adj.* showy; brightly colored. *Performers wear flamboyant costumes to attract attention.* —**flam•boy•ant•ly** *adv.* —**flam•boy•ance** *n.* —**flam•boy•an•cy** *n.*

**fore•cast**[1] /fôr′ kăst/ *n.* a prediction. *There is a forecast for snow later today.* —**fore•cast•er** *n.*

**fore•cast**[2] /fôr′ kăst/ *v.* **fore•cast** or **fore•cast•ed, fore•cast•ing, fore•casts.** to predict future happenings. *The economists forecast a stronger economy next year.* —**fore•cast•er** *n.*

**fo•ren•sic** /fə rĕn′ sĭk *or* fə rĕn′ zĭk/ *adj.* used in legal actions or for legal arguments. *Forensic science has helped to free many innocent people.* —**fo•ren•si•cal•ly** *adv.*

**for•mal•i•ty** /fôr măl′ ĭ tē/ *n., pl.* **for•mal•i•ties.** a strict following of established rules or customs. *Travel is a formality that is part of my job.*

**for•mal•ize** /fôr′ mə līz′/ *v.* **for•mal•ized, for•mal•iz•ing, for•mal•iz•es.** to give a definite or official form to (something). *The partners formalized their agreement by signing a contract.*

**fra•ter•nal**[1] /frə tûr′ nəl/ *adj.* pertaining to brothers. *The boys' mother ended their fraternal argument.* —**fra•ter•nal•ly** *adv.*

**fra•ter•nal**[2] /frə tûr′ nəl/ *adj.* brotherly. *The teammates have fraternal feelings for each other.* —**fra•ter•nal•ly** *adv.*

**fra•ter•ni•ty** /frə tûr′ nĭ tē/ *n., pl.* **fra•ter•ni•ties.** a group of people with something in common. *I belonged to a fraternity of business students in college.*

**frat•er•nize** /frăt′ ər nīz′/ *v.* **frat•er•nized, frat•er•niz•ing, frat•er•niz•es.** to associate with others in a brotherly or friendly way. *Do not fraternize with your opponent before the competition.*

**fu•gi•tive** /fyōō′ jĭ tĭv/ *n.* a person who escapes or flees. *The police are looking for the fugitive who robbed the bank.*

**fu•tile** /fyōōt′ l *or* fyōō′ tīl′/ *adj.* useless; hopeless. *It is futile to argue that we don't need homework.* —**fu•tile•ly** *adv.* —**fu•tile•ness** *n.*

## G

**gauge** /gāj/ *v.* **gauged, gaug•ing, gaug•es.** to estimate; to measure. *The farmer uses a bucket to gauge the monthly rainfall.*

## H

**hob•ble** /hŏb′ əl/ *v.* **hob•bled, hob•bling, hob•bles.** to limp or move with difficulty. *The injured athlete hobbled off the field.* —**hob•bler** *n.*

## I

**im•mu•ta•ble** /ĭ myōō′ tə bəl/ *adj.* unchangeable. *The laws of physics are immutable.*

---

<table>
<tr><th colspan="2">PRONUNCIATION KEY</th></tr>
<tr><td>/ă/</td><td>pat</td></tr>
<tr><td>/ā/</td><td>pay</td></tr>
<tr><td>/â/</td><td>care</td></tr>
<tr><td>/ä/</td><td>father</td></tr>
<tr><td>/är/</td><td>far</td></tr>
<tr><td>/ĕ/</td><td>pet</td></tr>
<tr><td>/ē/</td><td>be</td></tr>
<tr><td>/ĭ/</td><td>pit</td></tr>
<tr><td>/ī/</td><td>pie</td></tr>
<tr><td>/îr/</td><td>pier</td></tr>
<tr><td>/ŏ/</td><td>mop</td></tr>
<tr><td>/ō/</td><td>toe</td></tr>
<tr><td>/ô/</td><td>paw, for</td></tr>
<tr><td>/oi/</td><td>noise</td></tr>
<tr><td>/ou/</td><td>out</td></tr>
<tr><td>/ōō/</td><td>look</td></tr>
<tr><td>/ōō/</td><td>boot</td></tr>
<tr><td>/ŭ/</td><td>cut</td></tr>
<tr><td>/ûr/</td><td>urge</td></tr>
<tr><td>/th/</td><td>thin</td></tr>
<tr><td>/th/</td><td>this</td></tr>
<tr><td>/hw/</td><td>what</td></tr>
<tr><td>/zh/</td><td>vision</td></tr>
<tr><td>/ə/</td><td>about</td></tr>
<tr><td></td><td>item</td></tr>
<tr><td></td><td>pencil</td></tr>
<tr><td></td><td>gallop</td></tr>
<tr><td></td><td>circus</td></tr>
<tr><td>/ər/</td><td>butter</td></tr>
</table>

**im•par•tial** /ĭm pär′ shəl/ *adj.* fair; without bias. *A judge is impartial when he hears a case.* —**im•par•tial•ly** *adv.* —**im•par•ti•al•i•ty** *n.* —**im•par•tial•ness** *n.*

**im•plac•a•ble** /ĭm plăk′ ə bəl *or* ĭm plā′ kə bəl/ *adj.* determined; impossible to calm or pacify. *Her implacable nature made it impossible to reason with her.* —**im•plac•a•bly** *adv.* —**im•plac•a•bil•i•ty** *n.* —**im•plac•a•ble•ness** *n.*

**im•promp•tu** /ĭm prŏmp′ tōō *or* ĭm prŏmp′ tyōō/ *adj.* said or done without planning or preparing. *Let's have an impromptu party.*

**in•ces•sant** /ĭn sĕs′ ənt/ *adj.* never-ending; constant. *The fly's incessant buzz bothered me.* —**in•ces•sant•ly** *adv.*

**in•con•gru•ous** /ĭn kŏng′ grōō əs/ *adj.* not suitable; inappropriate or illogical. *The earmuffs seemed incongruous with the swimsuit he was wearing.* —**in•con•gru•ous•ly** *adv.* —**in•con•gru•ous•ness** *n.*

**in•cred•u•lous** /ĭn krĕj′ ə ləs/ *adj.* disbelieving. *Most people are incredulous of ghosts.* —**in•cred•u•lous•ly** *adv.* —**in•cred•u•lous•ness** *n.*

**in•cre•ment** /ĭn′ krə mənt/ *n.* one of a series of regular additions; an increase in the size of something. *We get new vocabulary words in increments of ten.* —**in•cre•men•tal** *adj.* —**in•cre•men•tal•ly** *adv.*

**in•doc•tri•nate** /ĭn dŏk′ trə nāt/ *v.* **in•doc•tri•nat•ed, in•doc•tri•nat•ing, in•doc•tri•nates.** to teach or instruct someone in the beliefs of a particular group. *The booklets will indoctrinate new members.* —**in•doc•tri•na•tion** *n.*

**in•duce•ment** /ĭn dōōs′ mənt/ *n.* an action aimed at persuading. *The store offered the coupon as an inducement to get us to buy the TV.*

**in•er•tia** /ĭ nûr′ shə/ *n.* the state of not moving or not feeling like moving. *I suffer from inertia when it is time to clean my room.* —**in•er•tial** *adj.* —**in•er•tial•ly** *adv.*

**in•frac•tion** /ĭn frăk′ shən/ *n.* the breaking of a rule. *We were punished for the infraction.*

**in•hab•i•tant** /ĭn hăb′ ĭ tənt/ *n.* a permanent resident. *After six months, she considered herself an inhabitant of the town.*

**in•hi•bi•tion** /ĭn′ hə bĭsh′ ən *or* ĭn′ ə bĭsh′ ən/ *n.* something that prevents a person from acting freely. *Jackie's inhibitions kept her from trying out for a part in the play.*

**in•ju•ri•ous** /ĭn jōŏr′ ē əs/ *adj.* harmful. *Too much time in the sun can be injurious to your health.* —**in•ju•ri•ous•ly** *adv.* —**in•ju•ri•ous•ness** *n.*

**in•sep•a•ra•ble** /ĭn sĕp′ ər ə bəl *or* ĭn sĕp′ rə bəl/ *adj.* cannot be separated. *The two girls are inseparable friends.* —**in•sep•a•ra•bly** *adv.* —**in•sep•a•ra•ble•ness** *n.*

**in•still** /ĭn stĭl′/ *v.* **in•stilled, in•still•ing, in•stills.** to introduce gradually; to implant. *Parents try to instill good values in their children.* —**in•stil•la•tion** *n.* —**in•still•er** *n.*

**in•ter•cede**[1] /ĭn′ tər sēd′/ *v.* **in•ter•ced•ed, in•ter•ced•ing, in•ter•cedes.** to speak for or plead on another's behalf. *Someone interceded for the innocent prisoner.*

**in•ter•cede**[2] /ĭn′ tər sēd′/ *v.* **in•ter•ced•ed, in•ter•ced•ing, in•ter•cedes.** to mediate in a dispute. *The coach had to intercede in the hockey players' argument.*

**in•ter•ces•sion** /ĭn′ tər sĕsh′ ən/ *n.* mediation in a dispute. *The teacher's intercession came just before James lost his temper.*

**in•ter•val**[1] /ĭn′ tər vəl/ *n.* the time between happenings. *We usually have math tests at ten-day intervals.*

**in•ter•val**[2] /ĭn′ tər vəl/ *n.* the distance between two line segments representing the time between happenings. *This interval on the timeline represents the Civil War.*

**in•trep•id** /ĭn trĕp′ ĭd/ *adj.* fearless and courageous. *The intrepid girls entered the haunted house.* —**in•trep•id•ly** *adv.* —**in•tre•pid•i•ty** *n.* —**in•trep•id•ness** *n.*

**in•tro•vert** /ĭn′ trə vûrt′/ *n.* a person who prefers to be alone. *Anita likes to study alone, but she is not an introvert.* —**in•tro•vert•ed** *adj.*

**i•rate** /ī rāt′/ *adj.* feeling very angry. *The irate man needed some time to cool his temper.* —**i•rate•ly** *adv.* —**i•rate•ness** *n.*

## J

**ju•ris•dic•tion** /jŏŏr′ ĭs dĭk′ shən/ *n.* legal authority; power. *The local court has jurisdiction in this case.*

## L

**la•ment** /lə mĕnt′/ *v.* **la•ment•ed, la•ment•ing, la•ments.** to express regret or sorrow; to mourn. *Ana lamented the loss of her grandfather.*

**lei•sure** /lē′ zhər *or* lĕzh′ ər/ *n.* a pleasurable activity done in one's free time. *Playing the guitar is a form of leisure for me.*

**le•ni•ent** /lē′ nē ənt *or* lēn′ yənt/ *adj.* not harsh or strict; merciful. *Mrs. Thompson is very lenient with her homework assignments.* —**le•ni•ent•ly** *adv.*

**leth•ar•gy** /lĕth′ ər jē/ *n., pl.* **leth•ar•gies.** physical or mental slowness. *Jarod's lethargy passed after a good night's sleep.*

**lev•i•ty** /lĕv′ ĭ tē/ *n., pl.* **lev•i•ties.** a light, humorous manner; playfulness, especially when inappropriate. *Levity during study period will not be tolerated.*

**li•a•ble¹** /lī′ ə bəl/ *adj.* legally responsible. *The person who caused the accident is liable for the damages.*

**li•a•ble²** /lī′ ə bəl/ *adj.* likely. *You are liable to slip on those icy stairs.*

**lock step¹** /lŏk′ stĕp′/ *n.* an inflexible procedure that cannot be changed. *We have to obey the lock step of the dress code.*

**lock step²** /lŏk′ stĕp′/ *n.* a type of marching in which the marchers follow each other as closely as possible in step. *The band marched in lock step.*

**lon•gev•i•ty** /lŏn jĕv′ ĭ tē *or* lôn jĕv′ ĭ tē/ *n., pl.* **lon•gev•i•ties.** a long life. *Longevity runs in his family, with many relatives living for 100 years.*

**lope** /lōp/ *v.* **loped, lop•ing, lopes.** to run in a relaxed and steady way. *The wolf loped along the snowy trail.*

## M

**mass** /măs/ *n.* a large accumulation of matter with no specific shape. *The mass of students poured into the auditorium.*

**me•an•der** /mē ăn′ dər/ *v.* **me•an•dered, me•an•der•ing, me•an•ders.** to roam or wander aimlessly. *They spent time meandering through the shopping mall.*

**me•di•ate** /mē′ dē āt′/ *v.* **me•di•at•ed, me•di•at•ing, me•di•ates.** to help opposing sides reach an agreement. *The counselor mediated an agreement between the two students.* —**me•di•ate•ly** *adv.*

**mil•len•ni•um** /mə lĕn′ ē əm/ *n., pl.* **mil•len•ni•ums** *or* **mil•len•ni•a** /mĭ lĕn′ ē ə/. a period of 1,000 years. *We recently entered the third millennium.* —**mil•len•ni•al** *adj.*

**mis•con•strue** /mĭs′ kən strōō′/ *v.* **mis•con•strued, mis•con•stru•ing, mis•con•strues.** to misunderstand; to misinterpret. *We'd better not misconstrue the teacher's instructions.*

**mod•er•ate** /mŏd′ ər ĭt/ *adj.* a reasonable amount; not extreme or excessive. *Hannah receives a moderate allowance.* —**mod•er•ate•ly** *adv.* —**mod•er•a•tion** *n.*

**mo•men•tum** /mō mĕn′ təm/ *n., pl.* **mo•men•ta** /mō mĕn′ tə/ *or* **mo•men•tums.** a force that keeps things moving. *We have the momentum to win the basketball championship.*

**mon•i•tor** /mŏn′ ĭ tər/ *v.* **mon•i•tored, mon•i•tor•ing, mon•i•tors.** to keep track of. *We monitored the progress of the hurricane.*

**mul•ti•tude** /mŭl′ tĭ tōōd′/ *n.* a large number. *The multitude of fans cheered for the winning team.*

## N

**non•con•form•ist** /nŏn′ kən fôr′ mĭst/ *n.* a person who refuses to follow accepted rules or customs. *The nonconformist refused to raise his hand when he wanted to speak.* —**non•con•form•i•ty** *n.*

<table>
<tr><td colspan="2">PRONUNCIATION KEY</td></tr>
<tr><td>/ă/</td><td>pat</td></tr>
<tr><td>/ā/</td><td>pay</td></tr>
<tr><td>/â/</td><td>care</td></tr>
<tr><td>/ä/</td><td>father</td></tr>
<tr><td>/är/</td><td>far</td></tr>
<tr><td>/ĕ/</td><td>pet</td></tr>
<tr><td>/ē/</td><td>be</td></tr>
<tr><td>/ĭ/</td><td>pit</td></tr>
<tr><td>/ī/</td><td>pie</td></tr>
<tr><td>/îr/</td><td>pier</td></tr>
<tr><td>/ŏ/</td><td>mop</td></tr>
<tr><td>/ō/</td><td>toe</td></tr>
<tr><td>/ô/</td><td>paw, for</td></tr>
<tr><td>/oi/</td><td>noise</td></tr>
<tr><td>/ou/</td><td>out</td></tr>
<tr><td>/ŏŏ/</td><td>look</td></tr>
<tr><td>/ōō/</td><td>boot</td></tr>
<tr><td>/ŭ/</td><td>cut</td></tr>
<tr><td>/ûr/</td><td>urge</td></tr>
<tr><td>/th/</td><td>thin</td></tr>
<tr><td>/th/</td><td>this</td></tr>
<tr><td>/hw/</td><td>what</td></tr>
<tr><td>/zh/</td><td>vision</td></tr>
<tr><td>/ə/</td><td>about</td></tr>
<tr><td></td><td>item</td></tr>
<tr><td></td><td>pencil</td></tr>
<tr><td></td><td>gallop</td></tr>
<tr><td></td><td>circus</td></tr>
<tr><td>/ər/</td><td>butter</td></tr>
</table>

## O

**ob•jec•tive** /əb jĕk′ tĭv/ *adj.* not influenced by personal prejudice; unbiased. *Members of the jury should be objective.* —**ob•jec•tive•ly** *adv.* —**ob•jec•tive•ness** *n.*

**o•dom•e•ter** /ō dŏm′ ĭ tər/ *n.* an instrument that measures distance traveled by a vehicle. *The odometer showed that we had traveled 3,200 miles.*

**out•spo•ken** /out spō′ kən/ *adj.* boldly frank and honest. *Suzanne always gives her outspoken opinion.* —**out•spo•ken•ly** *adv.* —**out•spo•ken•ness** *n.*

## P

**par•tial** /pär′ shəl/ *adj.* incomplete. *The witness gave a partial testimony.* —**par•tial•ness** *n.*

**par•ti•tion** /pär tĭsh′ ən/ *n.* a divider. *There is a partition between the two classrooms.*

**pa•tron•ize**[1] /pā′ trə nīz′ *or* păt′ rə nīz′/ *v.* **pa•tron•ized, pa•tron•iz•ing, pa•tron•iz•es.** to treat someone as if he were not as good as you; to be condescending. *Jack doesn't like it when his older brother patronizes him.* —**pa•tron•iz•ing•ly** *adv.*

**pa•tron•ize**[2] /pā′ trə nīz′ *or* păt′ rə nīz′/ *v.* **pa•tron•ized, pa•tron•iz•ing, pa•tron•iz•es.** to be a regular customer of. *We patronize the grocery store in our neighborhood.*

**peal**[1] /pēl/ *n.* a loud burst of noise. *We heard peals of laughter from the playground.*

**peal**[2] /pēl/ *v.* **pealed, peal•ing, peals.** to sound loudly; to ring. *The organ pealed out over the choir.*

**pe•dom•e•ter** /pĭ dŏm′ ĭ tər/ *n.* an instrument that measures distance walked. *I wore a pedometer on the hike.*

**per•en•ni•al**[1] /pə rĕn′ ē əl/ *adj.* happening again and again. *Our team is a perennial champion in softball.*

**per•en•ni•al**[2] /pə rĕn′ ē əl/ *n.* a plant that returns the next growing season. *Mom buys perennials for her flower garden.*

**per•fec•tion•ist** /pər fĕk′ shə nĭst/ *n.* a person who wants everything to be perfect. *Caitlin is such a perfectionist that she checks her homework three times.*

**pe•rim•e•ter** /pə rĭm′ ĭ tər/ *n.* the measurement around the outside border. *There was a fence around the perimeter of the field.* —**per•i•met•ric** /pĕr′ ə mĕt′ rĭk/ *adj.* —**per•i•met•ri•cal** *adj.* —**per•i•met•ri•cal•ly** *adv.*

**per•ju•ri•ous** /pər joŏr′ ē əs/ *adj.* marked by giving misleading or false testimony under oath in court. *The judge questioned the witness's perjurious comment.*

**per•ju•ry** /pûr′ jə rē/ *n., pl.* **per•ju•ries.** the giving of misleading or false testimony under oath in court. *To commit perjury is a serious offense.* —**per•ju•ri•ous•ly** *adv.*

**per•pe•trate** /pûr′ pə trāt′/ *v.* **per•pe•trat•ed, per•pe•trat•ing, per•pe•trates.** to commit. *Whoever perpetrated the crime will surely be caught.* —**per•pe•tra•tion** *n.* —**per•pe•tra•tor** *n.*

**per•pet•u•al**[1] /pər pĕch′ ōō əl/ *adj.* continuous. *My brother is in perpetual motion.* —**per•pet•u•al•ly** *adv.*

**per•pet•u•al**[2] /pər pĕch′ ōō əl/ *adj.* lasting forever. *The perpetual ice of Arctic glaciers is now threatened by global warming.* —**per•pet•u•al•ly** *adv.*

**per•turb** /pər tûrb′/ *v.* **per•turbed, per•turb•ing, per•turbs.** to bother greatly. *The loud noise perturbed the librarian.* —**per•turb•a•ble** *adj.*

**pho•net•ic** /fə nĕt′ ĭk/ *adj.* representing speech sounds with symbols. *The dictionary gives a phonetic spelling of each word.* —**pho•net•i•cal•ly** *adv.*

**pho•no•graph** /fō′ nə grăf′/ *n.* a record player. *People play records on a phonograph.*

**pla•cate** /plā′ kāt′ *or* plăk′ āt′/ *v.* **pla•cat•ed, pla•cat•ing, pla•cates.** to calm someone down by making concessions. *We had to placate the young child with a cookie.*

## Pronunciation Key

| PRONUNCIATION KEY | |
|---|---|
| /ă/ | pat |
| /ā/ | pay |
| /â/ | care |
| /ä/ | father |
| /är/ | far |
| /ĕ/ | pet |
| /ē/ | be |
| /ĭ/ | pit |
| /ī/ | pie |
| /îr/ | pier |
| /ŏ/ | mop |
| /ō/ | toe |
| /ô/ | paw, for |
| /oi/ | noise |
| /ou/ | out |
| /o͝o/ | look |
| /o͞o/ | boot |
| /ŭ/ | cut |
| /ûr/ | urge |
| /th/ | thin |
| /th/ | this |
| /hw/ | what |
| /zh/ | vision |
| /ə/ | about |
| | item |
| | pencil |
| | gallop |
| | circus |
| /ər/ | butter |

**plat•i•tude** /plăt′ ĭ to͞od′ or plăt′ i tyo͞od′/ *n.* a common, unoriginal remark. *My boss demanded fresh ideas, not just the same old platitudes.*

**pleas•ant•ry** /plĕz′ ən trē/ *n., pl.* **pleas•ant•ries.** a polite remark. *We exchanged pleasantries with the school principal.*

**pos•ter•i•ty** /pŏ stĕr′ ĭ tē/ *n.* future generations. *My aunt saves all of her family photos for posterity.*

**prec•e•dence** /prĕs′ ĭ dəns or prī sēd′ ns/ *n.* greater importance. *Studying for the test takes precedence over playing video games.*

**pred•i•cate** /prĕd′ ĭ kĭt′/ *n.* the part of the sentence that tells about the subject. *In the sentence "The girl walked slowly," the predicate is "walked slowly."*

**pre•dom•i•nant¹** /prī dŏm′ ə nənt/ *adj.* most important; main. *Professional football is the predominant sport among my friends.* —**pre•dom•i•nant•ly** *adv.*

**pre•dom•i•nant²** /prī dŏm′ ə nənt/ *adj.* most common. *Spanish is the predominant language studied in this high school.* —**pre•dom•i•nant•ly** *adv.*

**prel•ude¹** /prĕl′ yo͞od′ or prā′ lo͞od′ or prē′ lo͞od′/ *n.* an introductory event. *The dinner was a prelude to the formal dance.*

**prel•ude²** /prĕl′ yo͞od′ or prā′ lo͞od′ or prē′ lo͞od′/ *n.* the introduction to a musical piece. *People often recognize the prelude more than the major part of a symphony.*

**pre•sume** /prī zo͞om′/ *v.* **pre•sumed, pre•sum•ing, pre•sumes.** to take for granted. *We can't presume that we know everything.* —**pre•sum•ed•ly** *adv.* —**pre•sum•er** *n.*

**pri•me•val** /prī mē′ vəl/ *adj.* belonging to earliest times. *Dinosaurs used to roam the primeval forests.* —**pri•me•val•ly** *adv.*

**prim•i•tive** /prĭm′ ĭ tĭv/ *adj.* simple; not sophisticated. *The invention looks primitive, but it works.* —**prim•i•tive•ly** *adv.* —**prim•i•tive•ness** *n.*

**pri•mor•di•al¹** /prī môr′ dē əl/ *adj.* happening first. *Scientists study primordial life forms to understand their evolution.* —**pri•mor•di•al•ly** *adv.*

**pri•mor•di•al²** /prī môr′ dē əl/ *adj.* of fundamental importance. *Pronunciation plays a primordial role in learning a foreign language.* —**pri•mor•di•al•ly** *adv.*

**priv•y** /prĭv′ ē/ *adj.* sharing secret knowledge. *We were not privy to the contents of the letter.*

**pro•fi•cient** /prə fĭsh′ ənt/ *adj.* skilled at doing something. *The student is especially proficient at math.* —**pro•fi•cient•ly** *adv.*

**pro•hib•it** /prō hĭb′ ĭt/ *v.* **pro•hib•it•ed, pro•hib•it•ing, pro•hib•its.** to prevent. *Smoking is prohibited in hospitals.*

**pro•long** /prə lông′ or prə lŏng′/ *v.* **pro•longed, pro•long•ing, pro•longs.** to lengthen in duration. *Bad weather prolonged our wait before the plane would take off.*

**prom•e•nade¹** /prŏm′ ə nād′ or prŏm′ ə näd′/ *v.* **prom•e•nad•ed, prom•e•nad•ing, prom•e•nades.** to stroll; to take a leisurely walk. *Let's promenade around the park.*

**prom•e•nade²** /prŏm′ ə nād′ or prŏm′ ə näd′/ *n.* a leisurely stroll. *They took a promenade on the ship's deck.*

**pros•e•cu•tion** /prŏs′ ĭ kyo͞o′ shən/ *n.* the government attorneys who try a person accused of a crime. *The prosecution hopes to send the criminal to jail.*

**pro•to•col** /prō′ tə kôl′ or prō′ tə kŏl′/ *n.* the rules of behavior in ceremonious situations. *The embassy must stick to protocol when hosting foreign visitors.*

**pro•to•type** /prō′ tə tīp′/ *n.* the original model. *Engineers have improved upon the prototype of the jet engine.*

## R

**rash¹** /răsh/ *adj.* **rash•er, rash•est.** impulsive. *Brad's rash actions usually cause him to get in trouble with his parents.* —**rash•ly** *adv.* —**rash•ness** *n.*

**rash²** /răsh/ *n.* a skin eruption, such as chicken pox. *The doctor diagnosed her rash as a reaction to poison ivy.*

**rash³** /răsh/ *n.* an outbreak of many occurrences within a short period of time. *There has been a rash of burglaries in our neighborhood.*

**ra•tion¹** /răsh′ ən *or* rā′ shən/ *n.* a fixed amount (usually food) given to someone. *We received our ration of trail mix for the camping trip.*

**ra•tion²** /răsh′ ən *or* rā′ shən/ *v.* **ra•tioned, ra•tion•ing, ra•tions.** to give a fixed amount. *We rationed our water supply during the climb up the mountain.*

**rau•cous** /rô′ kəs/ *adj.* harsh; loud. *The raucous cheers at the football game were deafening.* —**rau•cous•ly** *adv.* —**rau•cous•ness** *n.*

**re•cede** /rĭ sēd′/ *v.* **re•ced•ed, re•ced•ing, re•cedes.** to move back from a level, point, or mark. *The water receded during the drought season.*

**re•ces•sion** /rĭ sĕsh′ ən/ *n.* the act of moving back. *We lose more beach with the recession of every wave.*

**rec•on•cile** /rĕk′ ən sīl′/ *v.* **rec•on•ciled, rec•on•cil•ing, rec•on•ciles.** to settle a dispute; to resolve. *The two friends reconciled after weeks of not speaking to each other.* —**rec•on•cil•i•a•to•ry** *adj.* —**rec•on•cile•ment** *n.* —**rec•on•cil•er** *n.* —**rec•on•cil•i•a•tion** *n.*

**re•form¹** /rĭ fôrm′/ *n.* a change for the better. *Education reform is a hot political topic.*

**re•form²** /rĭ fôrm′/ *v.* **re•formed, re•form•ing, re•forms.** to improve. *Joe must reform his study habits to get better grades.* —**re•form•er** *n.*

**re•fute** /rĭ fyo͞ot′/ *v.* **re•fut•ed, re•fut•ing, re•futes.** to prove to be false or wrong. *Lawyers try to refute the prosecutor's arguments.* —**re•fut•a•ble** *adj.* —**re•fut•a•bly** *adv.* —**re•fut•a•bil•i•ty** *n.* —**re•fut•er** *n.*

**re•ha•bil•i•tate** /rē′ hə bĭl′ ĭ tāt′/ *v.* **re•ha•bil•i•tat•ed, re•ha•bil•i•tat•ing, re•ha•bil•i•tates.** to help someone return to a normal or useful life. *The patient needs to rehabilitate after knee surgery.* —**re•ha•bil•i•ta•tive** *adj.* —**re•ha•bil•i•ta•tion** *n.*

**re•it•er•ate** /rē ĭt′ ə rāt′/ *v.* **re•it•er•at•ed, re•it•er•at•ing, re•it•er•ates.** to say something again; to repeat. *The math teacher reiterated the instructions before the test.*

**re•it•er•a•tion** /rē ĭt′ ə rā′ shən/ *n.* the act of repeating. *The constant reiteration of the lyrics forced me to remember the song.*

**re•ject** /rĭ jĕkt′/ *v.* **re•ject•ed, re•ject•ing, re•jects.** to throw out; to refuse. *My idea for a class activity was rejected.* —**re•jec•tive** *adj.* —**re•ject•er** *or* **re•jec•tor** *n.*

**rep•re•hen•si•ble** /rĕp′ rĭ hĕn′ sə bəl/ *adj.* deserving rebuke or blame. *The man's reprehensible deed will not go unpunished.* —**rep•re•hen•si•bly** *adv.* —**rep•re•hen•si•bil•i•ty** *n.* —**rep•re•hen•si•ble•ness** *n.*

**re•prieve¹** /rĭ prēv′/ *n.* temporary relief. *We have a two-week reprieve from school!*

**re•prieve²** /rĭ prēv′/ *n.* a postponement or cancellation of punishment. *The man's reprieve came before spending one day in jail.*

**re•prieve³** /rĭ prēv′/ *v.* **re•prieved, re•priev•ing, re•prieves.** to postpone or cancel punishment. *The principal reprieved the suspension until after exams.*

**re•proach¹** /rĭ prōch′/ *n.* criticism; blame. *The students' behavior was beyond reproach.* —**re•proach•a•ble** *adj.* —**re•proach•a•bly** *adv.* —**re•proach•a•ble•ness** *n.*

**re•proach²** /rĭ prōch′/ *v.* **re•proached, re•proach•ing, re•proach•es.** to blame; to express disapproval of. *My parents reproached me for coming home late.* —**re•proach•a•ble** *adj.* —**re•proach•a•bly** *adv.* —**re•proach•a•ble•ness** *n.*

**res•o•nate** /rĕz′ ə nāt′/ *v.* **res•o•nat•ed, res•o•nat•ing, res•o•nates.** to produce a loud, prolonged, or echoing sound. *The chimes resonated through the great hall.*

**res•ti•tu•tion** /rĕs′ tĭ to͞o′ shən *or* rĕs′ tĭ tyo͞o′ shən/ *n.* compensation for loss or injury. *The judge ordered restitution for all damages caused by the accident.*

**re•tal•i•ate** /rĭ tăl′ ē āt′/ *v.* **re•tal•i•at•ed, re•tal•i•at•ing, re•tal•i•ates.** to repay an injury or insult with a similar injury or insult. *Sean would not retaliate against the classmate who insulted him.* —**re•tal•i•a•tive** *adj.* —**re•tal•i•a•tion** *n.*

**re•tal•i•a•to•ry** /rĭ tăl′ ē ə tôr′ ē/ *adj.* marked by repaying an injury or insult with a similar injury or insult. *The army carried out a retaliatory action against the enemy.*

**ret•i•cent** /rĕt′ ĭ sənt/ *adj.* quiet; shy. *The reticent student dreads speaking in front of the class.* —**ret•i•cent•ly** *adv.*

**re•tort¹** /rĭ tôrt′/ *v.* **re•tort•ed, re•tort•ing, re•torts.** to reply in a sharp or witty way. *The musician gave an angry retort to the music critic.*

**re•tort²** /rĭ tôrt′ or rē′ tôrt′/ *n.* a quick, often sharp or witty, reply. *The teacher was surprised by the student's clever retort.*

**re•tract** /rĭ trăkt′/ *v.* **re•tract•ed, re•tract•ing, re•tracts.** to take back or withdraw. *The airline retracted its special fare offer.* —**re•tract•a•ble** *adj.*

**re•trac•tion** /rĭ trăk′ shən/ *n.* the act of taking back or withdrawing something. *The retraction of her statement did not make the controversy go away.*

**re•ver•ber•ate** /rĭ vûr′ bə rāt′/ *v.* **re•ver•ber•at•ed, re•ver•ber•at•ing, re•ver•ber•ates.** to echo or resound. *The sound of the slamming door reverberated through the house.*

**re•ver•ber•a•tion** /rĭ vûr′ bə rā′ shən/ *n.* the act or condition of an echo. *The reverberation of the alarm sounded in my ear.*

**re•ver•sion** /rĭ vûr′ zhən/ *n.* a return to a previous condition. *Reversion of the roads is necessary after the winter.*

**re•vert¹** /rĭ vûrt′/ *v.* **re•vert•ed, re•vert•ing, re•verts.** to go back to a previous condition. *Environmentalists would like to see mined lands revert to a natural state.* —**re•vert•i•ble** *adj.* —**re•ver•tive** *adj.* —**re•vert•er** *n.*

**re•vert²** /rĭ vûrt′/ *v.* **re•vert•ed, re•vert•ing, re•verts.** to go back to old habits. *When the electricity went out, we reverted to candles.* —**re•vert•i•ble** *adj.* —**re•ver•tive** *adj.* —**re•vert•er** *n.*

**rote¹** /rōt/ *n.* memorization through repetition and without full comprehension. *Suzanne has learned the theory by rote but doesn't fully understand it.*

**rote²** /rōt/ *adj.* learned by memorization through repetition and without full comprehension. *His rote knowledge of the map did not help him find the store in the dark.*

**saun•ter¹** /sôn′ tər/ *v.* **saun•tered, saun•ter•ing, saun•ters.** to walk at an unhurried pace. *The boys sauntered over to the playground.*

**saun•ter²** /sôn′ tər/ *n.* a slow walk. *A saunter along the beach is relaxing.*

**scant•y** /skăn′ tē/ *adj.* **scant•i•er, scant•i•est.** small; limited in quantity. *Our food ration was unusually scanty.* —**scant•i•ly** *adv.* —**scant•i•ness** *n.*

**sed•en•tar•y** /sĕd′ n tĕr′ ē/ *adj.* sitting most of the time; not moving. *A sedentary job can cause you to gain weight.* —**sed•en•tar•i•ly** *adv.* —**sed•en•tar•i•ness** *n.*

**seg•re•ga•tion** /sĕg′ rĭ gā′ shən/ *n.* the separation from. *Segregation of the races is not beneficial to anyone.*

**se•quence** /sē′ kwəns or sē′ kwĕns′/ *n.* the order of things. *After 1, 3, and 5, the next number in the sequence is 7.*

**si•mul•ta•ne•ous** /sī′ məl tā′ nē əs or sĭm′ əl tā′ nē əs/ *adj.* happening or done at the same time. *A computer can perform many simultaneous actions.* —**si•mul•ta•ne•ous•ly** *adv.* —**si•mul•ta•ne•ous•ness** *n.*

**sin•is•ter** /sĭn′ ĭ stər/ *adj.* threatening evil. *The sinister prince was hoping to fool the princess.* —**sin•is•ter•ly** *adv.* —**sin•is•ter•ness** *n.*

<table>
<tr><td colspan="2">PRONUNCIATION KEY</td></tr>
<tr><td>/ă/</td><td>pat</td></tr>
<tr><td>/ā/</td><td>pay</td></tr>
<tr><td>/â/</td><td>care</td></tr>
<tr><td>/ä/</td><td>father</td></tr>
<tr><td>/är/</td><td>far</td></tr>
<tr><td>/ĕ/</td><td>pet</td></tr>
<tr><td>/ē/</td><td>be</td></tr>
<tr><td>/ĭ/</td><td>pit</td></tr>
<tr><td>/ī/</td><td>pie</td></tr>
<tr><td>/îr/</td><td>pier</td></tr>
<tr><td>/ŏ/</td><td>mop</td></tr>
<tr><td>/ō/</td><td>toe</td></tr>
<tr><td>/ô/</td><td>paw, for</td></tr>
<tr><td>/oi/</td><td>noise</td></tr>
<tr><td>/ou/</td><td>out</td></tr>
<tr><td>/o͞o/</td><td>look</td></tr>
<tr><td>/o͞o/</td><td>boot</td></tr>
<tr><td>/ŭ/</td><td>cut</td></tr>
<tr><td>/ûr/</td><td>urge</td></tr>
<tr><td>/th/</td><td>thin</td></tr>
<tr><td>/th/</td><td>this</td></tr>
<tr><td>/hw/</td><td>what</td></tr>
<tr><td>/zh/</td><td>vision</td></tr>
<tr><td>/ə/</td><td>about</td></tr>
<tr><td></td><td>item</td></tr>
<tr><td></td><td>pencil</td></tr>
<tr><td></td><td>gallop</td></tr>
<tr><td></td><td>circus</td></tr>
<tr><td>/ər/</td><td>butter</td></tr>
</table>

**so•journ¹** /sō′ jûrn′ *or* sō jûrn′/ *v.* **so•journed, so•journ•ing, so•journs.** to stay for a while. *We will sojourn in San Francisco.* —**so•journ•er** *n.*

**so•journ²** /sō′ jûrn′ *or* sō jûrn′/ *n.* a temporary stay during travel. *We learned a lot about tribal customs during our sojourn in Africa.* —**so•journ•er** *n.*

**sol•i•dar•i•ty** /sŏl′ ĭ dăr′ ĭ tē/ *n.* an association with others for a common cause. *Unions work in solidarity to improve workers' conditions.*

**so•no•rous** /sə nôr′ əs *or* sŏn′ ər əs/ *adj.* having a rich, clear sound. *The sonorous voices of the choir thrilled the audience.* —**so•no•rous•ly** *adv.* —**so•no•rous•ness** *n.*

**stan•dard** /stăn′ dərd/ *adj.* commonly used or accepted; customary. *We followed standard rules of safety during the storm.*

**sta•tis•tics** /stə tĭs′ tĭks/ *n. (used with a singular verb)* the science that collects and studies data. *Statistics is one of my most difficult classes.*

**sta•tus¹** /stā′ təs *or* stăt′ əs/ *n., pl.* **sta•tus•es.** the state or condition at a particular time. *What is the status of your science project that is due next week?*

**sta•tus²** /stā′ təs *or* stăt′ əs/ *n., pl.* **sta•tus•es.** prestige. *Members of Congress have a position of status in our country.*

**stat•ute** /stăch′ ōot/ *n.* a law enacted by a legislature. *The state Senate enacted the statute last year.*

**stat•u•to•ry** /stăch′ ə tôr′ ē/ *adj.* relating to a law enacted by a legislature. *The statutory age for driving is sixteen.*

**stim•u•lus** /stĭm′ yə ləs/ *n., pl.* **stim•u•li** /stĭm′ yə lī′/. something that causes a response. *The smells from the kitchen are a great stimulus to my appetite.*

**strain¹** /strān/ *n.* a musical passage. *We heard the strains of my favorite song.*

**strain²** /strān/ *n.* physical or mental stress. *Studying for exams is a big strain.*

**strain³** /strān/ *v.* **strained, strain•ing, strains.** to work very hard. *The child strained to reach the toy on the top shelf.*

**stren•u•ous** /strĕn′ yōo əs/ *adj.* requiring a lot of energy or effort. *Digging ditches is a strenuous job.* —**stren•u•ous•ly** *adv.* —**stren•u•ous•ness** *n.*

**sub•due** /səb dōo′ *or* səb dyōo′/ *v.* **sub•dued, sub•du•ing, sub•dues.** to control or restrain physically; to calm down. *The police arrived to subdue the two angry men.*

**sub•dued** /səb dōod′ *or* səb dyōod′/ *adj.* restrained; quiet. *Her subdued behavior made us think something was wrong.*

**sub•jec•tive** /səb jĕk′ tĭv/ *adj.* related to a particular person's point of view. *The writer's review of the new restaurant was entirely subjective.* —**sub•jec•tive•ly** *adv.* —**sub•jec•tive•ness** *n.*

**sub•lime** /sə blīm′/ *adj.* impressive; awe-inspiring. *The view of the Grand Canyon is sublime.* —**sub•lime•ly** *adv.*

**sub•se•quent** /sŭb′ sĭ kwĕnt′ *or* sŭb′ sĭ kwənt′/ *adj.* following in time or order; later. *The teacher's subsequent tests will get harder.* —**sub•se•quent•ly** *adv.* —**sub•se•quent•ness** *n.*

**sub•stan•tial** /səb stăn′ shəl/ *adj.* a large amount or size. *Our class gave a substantial donation to the zoo.* —**sub•stan•tial•ly** *adv.* —**sub•stan•tial•ness** *n.*

**sub•ver•sive** /səb vûr′ sĭv *or* səb vûr′ zĭv/ *adj.* meant to overthrow or undermine. *Luckily, the subversive plot failed.* —**sub•ver•sive•ly** *adv.* —**sub•ver•sive•ness** *n.*

**suc•cinct** /sək sĭngkt′/ *adj.* brief; stated in few words. *Be succinct in your writing.* —**suc•cinct•ly** *adv.* —**suc•cinct•ness** *n.*

**sup•pli•cant** /sŭp′ lĭ kənt/ *n.* a person who humbly or earnestly asks for something. *The supplicant asked the court to award him damages.*

**sur•mise** /sər mīz′/ *v.* **sur•mised, sur•mis•ing, sur•mis•es.** to suppose; to infer from evidence. *Some scientists surmise that there might have been life on Mars at one time.*

**sur•rep•ti•tious** /sûr′ əp tĭsh′ əs/ *adj.* secretive. *Johnny's surreptitious actions made his teacher suspicious.* —**sur•rep•ti•tious•ly** *adv.* —**sur•rep•ti•tious•ness** *n.*

**sur•veil•lance** /sər **vā′** ləns/ *n.* the close observation of a person or group. *The detective had the man under surveillance.*

**sym•me•try** /**sĭm′** ĭ trē/ *n., pl.* **sym•me•tries.** the balance achieved when opposite sides have the same size, shape, and position. *The landscaper achieved perfect symmetry with the rose garden.*

**sym•pho•ny**[1] /**sĭm′** fə nē/ *n., pl.* **sym•pho•nies.** a large orchestra. *The symphony will have a guest conductor tonight.*

**sym•pho•ny**[2] /**sĭm′** fə nē/ *n., pl.* **sym•pho•nies.** the music written for a symphony orchestra. *Beethoven wrote many symphonies in his lifetime.*

**syn•chro•nize** /**sĭng′** krə nīz′ *or* **sĭn′** krə nīz′/ *v.* **syn•chro•nized, syn•chro•niz•ing, syn•chro•niz•es.** to cause to happen at the same time. *The swimmers synchronized their moves.* —**syn•chro•ni•za•tion** *n.*

---

**T**

**ten•den•cy** /**tĕn′** dən sē/ *n., pl.* **ten•den•cies.** a leaning; a likelihood that is characteristic of someone or something. *Unfortunately, Dad has a tendency to react first and ask questions later.*

**terse** /tûrs/ *adj.* **ters•er, ters•est.** brief and to the point. *The cab driver's terse response was a welcome change.* —**terse•ly** *adv.* —**terse•ness** *n.*

**ther•a•peu•tic** /**thĕr′** ə pyoo′ tĭk/ *adj.* curing; healing. *Exercise can be very therapeutic.* —**ther•a•peu•ti•cal•ly** *adv.*

**thwart** /thwôrt/ *v.* **thwart•ed, thwart•ing, thwarts.** to block or prevent; to frustrate. *The basketball team's defense thwarted their opponent's efforts to score.*

**traipse** /trāps/ *v.* **traipsed, traips•ing, traips•es.** to walk or tramp about. *The children traipse through the puddles.*

**tran•scend** /trăn **sĕnd′**/ *v.* **tran•scend•ed, tran•scend•ing, tran•scends.** to go past the limits of. *Her math skills transcend those of typical 8th graders.*

**trans•gres•sion** /trăns **grĕsh′** ən *or* trănz **grĕsh′** ən/ *n.* an instance of breaking the law or going against a command. *Lying in a court of law is a serious transgression.*

**tra•verse** /trə **vûrs′** *or* **trăv′** ərs/ *v.* **tra•versed, tra•vers•ing, tra•vers•es.** to travel across. *Steve Fossett tried to traverse the globe in a hot air balloon.*

**tread**[1] /trĕd/ *v.* **trod** /trŏd/, **tread•ing, treads.** to walk on or over. *We tread the same path to school every day.*

**tread**[2] /trĕd/ *v.* **trod** /trŏd/, **tread•ing, treads.** to trample on something. *We shouldn't tread on the grass.*

**tur•bu•lent**[1] /**tûr′** byə lənt/ *adj.* violently disturbed or agitated. *The turbulent waters of the Mississippi caused much destruction.* —**tur•bu•lent•ly** *adv.*

**tur•bu•lent**[2] /**tûr′** byə lənt/ *adj.* causing unrest or disturbance. *His turbulent behavior was frightening.* —**tur•bu•lent•ly** *adv.*

**tur•moil** /**tûr′** moil′/ *n.* great confusion or agitation. *The turmoil of war upset the lives of everyone.*

---

**U**

**ul•ti•ma•tum** /**ŭl′** tə **mā′** təm *or* **ŭl′** tə **mā′** təm/ *n., pl.* **ul•ti•ma•tums** *or* **ul•ti•ma•ta** /**ŭl′** tə **mā′** tə *or* **ŭl′** tə **mā′** tə/. a statement of terms; a threat; a final warning. *My parents issued an ultimatum: clean my room or else.*

---

**V**

**vag•a•bond** /**văg′** ə bŏnd′/ *n.* a wanderer, usually homeless. *The shelter helps vagabonds.*

**val•e•dic•to•ri•an** /**văl′** ĭ dĭk **tôr′** ē ən/ *n.* the student at the top of the class who gives a speech at graduation. *The valedictorian gave a compelling speech for her classmates.*

**ver•sa•tile**[1] /**vûr′** sə təl *or* **vûr′** sə tīl′/ *adj.* able to do many things well. *Our band director is very versatile.* —**ver•sa•tile•ly** *adv.* —**ver•sa•tile•ness** *n.* —**ver•sa•til•i•ty** *n.*

---

### PRONUNCIATION KEY

| | |
|---|---|
| /ă/ | p**a**t |
| /ā/ | p**a**y |
| /â/ | c**a**re |
| /ä/ | f**a**ther |
| /är/ | f**ar** |
| /ĕ/ | p**e**t |
| /ē/ | b**e** |
| /ĭ/ | p**i**t |
| /ī/ | p**ie** |
| /îr/ | p**ier** |
| /ŏ/ | m**o**p |
| /ō/ | t**oe** |
| /ô/ | p**aw**, f**or** |
| /oi/ | n**oi**se |
| /ou/ | **ou**t |
| /oo/ | l**oo**k |
| /ōō/ | b**oo**t |
| /ŭ/ | c**u**t |
| /ûr/ | **ur**ge |
| /th/ | **th**in |
| /*th*/ | **th**is |
| /hw/ | **wh**at |
| /zh/ | vi**s**ion |
| /ə/ | **a**bout |
| | it**e**m |
| | penc**i**l |
| | gall**o**p |
| | circ**u**s |
| /ər/ | butt**er** |

**ver•sa•tile²** /vûr′ sə təl *or* vûr′ sə tīl′/ *adj.* having many uses or functions. *The most versatile of books is the dictionary.* —**ver•sa•tile•ly** *adv.* —**ver•sa•tile•ness** *n.* —**ver•sa•til•i•ty** *n.*

**ver•sus** /vûr′ səs *or* vûr′ səz/ *prep.* against. *The championship game will feature Springfield versus Middletown.*

**vile¹** /vīl/ *adj.* **vil•er, vil•est.** hateful; evil. *The criminal was sent to prison for his vile deeds.* —**vile•ly** *adv.* —**vile•ness** *n.*

**vile²** /vīl/ *adj.* **vil•er, vil•est.** disgusting. *A vile and slimy creature lives in the swamp.* —**vile•ly** *adv.* —**vile•ness** *n.*

**vo•cif•er•ous** /vō sĭf′ ər əs/ *adj.* noisy; making an outcry. *The vociferous crowd wouldn't let the president speak.* —**vo•cif•er•ous•ly** *adv.*

**way•ward** /wā′ wərd/ *adj.* disobedient. *She is a wayward child.*

# Word Wisdom Index

**Cover Illustration:** Dave Cutler

**Photo and Illustration Credits:** Page 6, 28, PhotoDisc; 46, Bob Horvath; 50, PhotoSpin; 72, Clipart.com; 94, Eyewire Images; 116, Clipart.com; 138, PhotoSpin; 160, 182, Clipart.com

**Borders and Icons:** Brock Waldron

**Context Clues Strategies:** Adapted from Camille Blachowicz and Peter J. Fisher. *Teaching Vocabulary in All Classrooms.* (2002). New Jersey: Merrill/Prentice Hall. p. 26

Printed in the United States of America